HOW TO PASS

THE QTS NUMERACY SKILLS TEST

HOW TO PASS

THE QTS NUMERACY SKILLS TEST

Essential maths and statistics practice for the Qualified Teacher Status skills test

CHRIS TYREMAN

Publisher's note

Every possible effort has been made to ensure that the information contained in this book is accurate at the time of going to press, and the publishers and authors cannot accept responsibility for any errors or omissions, however caused. No responsibility for loss or damage occasioned to any person acting, or refraining from action, as a result of the material in this publication can be accepted by the editor, the publisher or any of the authors.

First published in Great Britain in 2009 by Kogan Page Limited

Kogan Page Limited
120 Pentonville Road
London N1 9JN
United Kingdom
www.koganpage.com

British Library Cataloguing in Publication Data

A CIP record for this book is available from the British Library.

ISBN 978 0 7494 5460 9

Typeset by Saxon Graphics Ltd, Derby
Printed and bound in India by Replika Press Pvt Ltd

Contents

Introduction

All trainee teachers seeking Qualified Teacher Status (QTS) must pass the Numeracy Skills Test, the Literacy Skills Test and the ICT Skills Test. This book will enable you to pass the Numeracy Skills Test at your first attempt. Of course it cannot, without some effort, miraculously pass the test for you, but if you work steadily through each chapter you can succeed.

The pass mark in the QTS Numeracy Skills Test is 17 correct answers out of 28 questions (60 per cent) and whilst this is not very high, candidates who work too slowly will not pass. For this reason, the first chapter teaches quick ways of answering the mental arithmetic questions. Five mock QTS mental arithmetic tests of 12 questions each provide plenty of practice.

The remaining two chapters cover the general arithmetic and statistical skills required for the 'on-screen' questions. Two mock 'on-screen' QTS-type tests complete the book, which comes with worked-through answers.

Each chapter begins with a 'maths audit' so you can review the exact skills required for each section of the test. To interpret the questions you must be able convert the language of the questions into mathematical operations, as per the following example:

A comprehensive school has 1,400 pupils on roll, including 154 A-level students. What percentage of the pupils on roll are A-level students?

The arithmetic required is division followed by multiplication:

154 ÷ 1400 × 100%

All the material in this book comes with expanded answers that show the calculations.

Whilst you need only to remember the four arithmetic operations of addition (+), subtraction (–), multiplication (×) and division (÷), you should be familiar with the different ways that these operations can be denoted in question form, as given here:

(×) multiply by, times, lots of, product, twice, double, half, multiple, fraction;
(÷) divide by, proportion, ratio, per/percent, out of, each, scale, factor;
(+) add, total, plus, sum, tally, more than;
(–) subtract, difference, take, less than.

To interpret the graphs you must be able to work out the distance from one tick mark to the next along the axis, ie divide the scale by the number of tick mark intervals, as per the examples shown below.

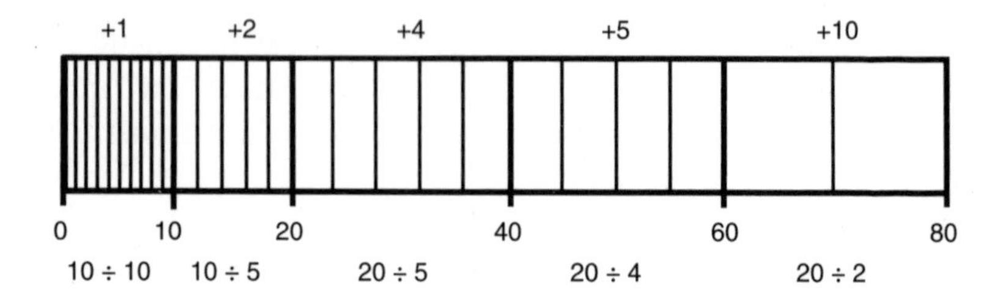

Why students fail the QTS tests

Candidates who fail the test tend to do so for the following reasons.

Lack of knowledge

This is probably the main reason why students fail. As a guide, you should have at least a grade B in GCSE maths if you expect to pass the test without preparing for it. If you managed only a grade C or lower then you must prepare carefully. This book will help you whatever your level because it assumes that you have forgotten much of what you learnt at school or college, or that you never understood it in the first place. It builds on your existing knowledge by using graded exercises combined with fully explained answers. Mock tests are included to simulate the live test experience as far as possible.

Time pressure

Time constraints are another key reason why candidates fail. The test lasts 48 minutes with 12 minutes for the mental arithmetic questions and 36 minutes for the longer on-screen questions. The mental arithmetic questions are the most troublesome because each question has a strict time limit. If you are only halfway through a question when the next question is read out then you cannot put up your hand and ask the questioner to wait! With the on-screen questions you can work at your own pace, even if the penalty is missing out on answering every question. It is better to be certain of a few correct answers than to guess too many, leaving everything to chance.

Another tip for improving your mark is to increase the speed of your calculations. This book explains ways in which this can be done. Do not attempt to work out every problem mentally, but instead use the pencil and paper provided to write down most of the steps in a calculation. You are far more likely to make numerical errors if you rely too heavily on your memory. For the purposes of the QTS test, mental arithmetic is not about working everything out in your head, it is arithmetic without the help of a calculator.

Maths phobia

This is the third reason why people fail. Test takers with a mental block on maths are susceptible to panic attacks before or during the test and this can lead to repeated failures. Fortunately for these people, there is no limit on the number of times they can attempt to pass the QTS tests and gain Qualified Teacher Status. This third reason for lack of test success is really a combination of the first two, ie a lack of knowledge and an inability to cope with the pressure of working against the clock. A vicious circle of anxiety and a lack of understanding ensue to create even more anxiety with feelings of hopelessness.

If this happens to you, then stop, put down your pencil, close your eyes, take a few deep breaths, then open your eyes and start again. Maths phobia can be overcome by practising your maths skills daily until you feel more confident.

Calculator skills

The calculator and the on-screen nature of the test can be off-putting for some people. You should not have to rely on the on-screen calculator for every single step of the on-screen questions, but you do need to make sure that you are confident with a calculator for the times when it is required.

The QTS on-screen calculator is a basic arithmetic calculator rather than a scientific type. This means that it will only cope with single step arithmetic processes. Eg, 250 ÷ 1.6 can be worked out by simply using the mouse to click on:

[2] [5] [0] [÷] [1] [.] [6] [=]

However, 250 ÷ 1.6 + 2.75 must be manually split into two parts:

250 ÷ 1.6 = 156.25

Write the answer down, then click on [C] to clear the answer and use the mouse to enter 156.25 + 2.75 as a final step:

[1] [5] [6] [.] [2] [5] [+] [2] [.] [7] [5]

The [CE] key can be used to clear the last entry if you make a mistake, but it is often better to use the [C] key and start the calculation afresh.

Finally, you can click on the blue bar at the head of the calculator to drag it to a more convenient position on the screen.

TDA website

You can register for the QTS skills tests via the following web address: www.tda.gov.uk/skillstests.aspx (or type 'QTS' into the Google search engine). To book a test you will need a registration number issued to you by your training provider. Full details of where to take the tests are available from the TDA website, which also includes links to on-line practice tests. You can book all three QTS tests for the same day, depending on availability. Your test results will be shown on-screen as soon as you have finished the test.

Men are disturbed, not by things, but by the views and notions which they form concerning things. When we are hindered, let us never attribute it to others, but to ourselves; that is, to our own principles. A person lacking information or instruction will lay the fault of his own bad condition upon others. Someone just starting instruction will lay the fault on himself. Someone who is well informed and instructed will place blame neither on others nor on himself.

Epictetus (55 AD)

1

Mental arithmetic

Maths audit 1

For the mental arithmetic section you need to know the following.

Whole numbers

- How to add, subtract, multiply and divide whole numbers.
- How to multiply by or divide by 10, 100, 1000, etc.
- How to break down large numbers by finding the prime factors.

Fractions, proportions and ratios

- How to add and subtract fractions with the same and different denominators (find a common denominator).
- How to multiply fractions together (multiply the top numbers and the bottom numbers).
- How to divide fractions (turn the right-hand fraction upside-down and multiply as for multiplications).

- How to work with improper (top-heavy) fractions (same rules apply).
- How to work with mixed fractions (whole number + fraction) by converting to an improper fraction as a first step.
- How to cancel fractions (equivalent fractions) and cross-cancel fractions when multiplying fractions together.
- How to divide quantities into ratios and proportional parts.

Decimal numbers

- How to add and subtract decimal numbers (same as for whole numbers but keep the decimal points aligned).
- How to multiply decimals by 10, 100, 1000, etc (move the decimal point to the right by how many zeros you have).
- How to divide decimals by 10, 100, 1000, etc (move the decimal point to the left by how many zeros you have).
- How to multiply decimals by ordinary numbers (multiply as normal and then remember: number of decimal places in the question = number of decimal places in the answer).
- How to divide decimals by ordinary numbers (divide as normal keeping the decimal point in the same position).
- How to divide by decimal numbers (change the decimal into a whole number as a first step).
- How to convert decimals into fractions and vice versa.

Percentages

- How to express a percentage as a fraction with a denominator of 100.
- How to write a percentage as a decimal by dividing by 100.

- How to multiply any number by any percentage using either a fractions method or a decimals method.
- How to work out a percentage change (increase or decrease).

Time

How to express time using the 24-hour clock, and how to calculate time intervals, and find start and end times.

Money

How to work with the decimal system and exchange rates.

Working with whole numbers

Traditional methods of calculation are too slow for the QTS mental arithmetic questions so this chapter reviews short-cut techniques that save time. However, you still need to memorize the multiplication table.

Table 1.1 Multiplication table (try to memorize it)

	1	2	3	4	5	6	7	8	9	10	11	12
1	1	2	3	4	5	6	7	8	9	10	11	12
2	2	4	6	8	10	12	14	16	18	20	22	24
3	3	6	9	12	15	18	21	24	27	30	33	36
4	4	8	12	16	20	24	28	32	36	40	44	48
5	5	10	15	20	25	30	35	40	45	50	55	60
6	6	12	18	24	30	36	42	48	54	60	66	72
7	7	14	21	28	35	42	49	56	63	70	77	84
8	8	16	24	32	40	48	56	64	72	80	88	96
9	9	18	27	36	45	54	63	72	81	90	99	108
10	10	20	30	40	50	60	70	80	90	100	110	120
11	11	22	33	44	55	66	77	88	99	110	121	132
12	12	24	36	48	60	72	84	96	108	120	132	144

Whole numbers have a *place-value* based on the decimal system of units, tens, hundreds and thousands, etc. Large numbers can be added and subtracted by splitting them into building blocks based on place values. For example:

$9537 = (9 \times 1000) + (5 \times 100) + (3 \times 10) + (7 \times 1)$
$= 9000 + 500 + 30 + 7$

Similarly: $6142 = 6000 + 100 + 40 + 2$

9537 and 6142 can added from left to right, starting with the largest place-value (thousands):

$9537 + 6142 = 15000 + 600 + 70 + 9 = 15679$

9537 can be multiplied in a similar way, for example by 3:

$9537 \times 3 = 9000 \times 3 + 500 \times 3 + 30 \times 3 + 7 \times 3$
$= 27000 + 1500 + 90 + 21 = 28000 + 590 + 21 = 28611$

Subtraction of large numbers is best carried out by subtracting a larger quantity than you need to initially; typically hundred(s) or thousand(s) and then adding back the difference. For example:

$927 - 68 = 927 - 100 + 32 = 827 + 32 = 859$

Similarly: $2350 - 185 = 2350 - 200 + 15 = 2150 + 15 = 2165$

Division can be simplified by breaking numbers down according to place-value. Brackets have been included for clarity. For example:

$864 \div 4 = (800 \div 4) + (60 \div 4) + (4 \div 4)$
$= 200 + 15 + 1 = 216$

$168 \div 12 = (120 \div 12) + (48 \div 12) = 10 + 4 = 14$

Method:

i) split 168 into 120 and 48 because it is much easier to divide 120 by 12 and 48 by 12 than it is to divide 168 by 12;
ii) divide 120 by 12 to give 10;
iii) divide 48 by 12 to give 4;
iv) add the two results: $10 + 4 = 14$.

Instead of splitting the number, you can also add to it if this makes the division easier, then subtract at the end to compensate. For example:

$$168 \div 12 = (180 \div 12) - (12 \div 12) = 15 - 1 = 14$$

Method:

i) add 12 to 168 to give 180;
ii) divide 180 by 12 to give 15 ($15 \times 12 = 150 + 30 = 180$);
ii) divide 12 (the amount added on in step i)) by 12 to give 1;
iii) subtract 1 from 15 to give: $15 - 1 = 14$.

The following rules are helpful when dividing:

i) if the last digit is 0, 2,4, 6, or 8, the number will divide by 2;
ii) if the last digit ends in 0 or 5 the number will divide by 5;
ii) if the last digit ends in 0 the number will divide by 10;
ii) if the last two digits divide by 4 the number will divide by 4 (eg 128, 132, 136, 240, 244, 348, 552, 760, 964, 1012).

You can break down (factorize) large numbers by dividing them by prime numbers. A *prime number* is a number that is divisible by only itself and 1. The first six prime numbers are 2, 3, 5, 7, 11 and 13. Start with the smallest of these (2) and continue with it if possible, otherwise try the next prime number (3). For example:

252 can be factorized as follows:

$252 \div 2 = 126$	$(250 \div 2) + (2 \div 2) = 125 + 1$
$126 \div 2 = 63$	$(120 \div 2) + (6 \div 2) = 60 + 3$
$63 \div 3 = 21$	$(60 \div 3) + (3 \div 3) = 20 + 1$
$21 \div 3 = 7$	

$252 = 2 \times 2 \times 3 \times 3 \times 7$

Knowledge of factors and prime numbers is useful for breaking down (factorizing) large numbers and for cancelling fractions.

Fractions

To cancel (simplify) fractions you divide the numerator (top number) and the denominator (bottom number) by the same prime factors (2, 3, 5, etc) to give the *equivalent fractions*. For example:

Cancel $\frac{6}{14}$ to its *lowest terms*

Method: divide 6 by 2 and divide 14 by 2 to give: $\frac{6}{14} = \frac{3}{7}$

Here are some examples:

$\frac{32}{36} = \frac{16}{18} = \frac{8}{9}$ (divide the top/bottom by 2 and then 2 again).

$\frac{18}{48} = \frac{9}{24} = \frac{3}{8}$ (divide the top/bottom by 2 and then by 3).

$\frac{45}{75} = \frac{9}{15} = \frac{3}{5}$ (divide the top/bottom by 5 and then by 3).

Addition and subtraction of fractions

If the denominators are the same you write the denominator once and add (or subtract) the two top numbers. For example:

$$\frac{2}{7} + \frac{3}{7} = \frac{5}{7}$$

If the denominators are different you need to find a common denominator that both denominators will divide into. For example:

$$\frac{1}{6} + \frac{3}{8}$$

A common denominator is a number that both 6 and 8 will divide into. There are many such numbers; the most obvious is 48 (6 × 8). However, there may be a lower common denominator that will make the working easier. One method of finding it is to write down the equivalent fractions that can be found by multiplying by prime numbers:

$$\frac{1}{6} = \frac{2}{12} = \frac{3}{18} = \frac{4}{24} = \frac{8}{48}$$

$$\frac{3}{8} = \frac{6}{16} = \frac{9}{24} = \frac{18}{48}$$

The lowest common denominator is 24, so:

$$\frac{1}{6} + \frac{3}{8} = \frac{4}{24} + \frac{9}{24} = \frac{13}{24}$$

The above fraction cannot be cancelled any further because 13 is a prime number. Subtraction of fractions is carried out in the same way.

Multiplication and division of fractions

To multiply fractions all you do is multiply the two numerators (top numbers) together and the two denominators (bottom numbers) together. For example:

$$\frac{1}{6} \times \frac{3}{8} = \frac{1 \times 3}{6 \times 8} = \frac{3}{48} = \frac{1}{16}$$

Division of fractions is similar, except that the fraction on the right-hand side must be turned upside down and then multiplied with the fraction on the left-hand side. For example:

$$\frac{1}{6} \div \frac{3}{8} \text{ becomes } \frac{1}{6} \times \frac{8}{3} = \frac{8}{18} = \frac{4}{9}$$

Improper fractions are top heavy with the numerator greater than the denominator. These fractions are added, subtracted, multiplied and divided in exactly the same way as for proper fractions. For example:

$$\frac{9}{4}+\frac{7}{3}=\frac{27}{12}+\frac{28}{12}=\frac{55}{12}\text{; then }\frac{55}{12}=\frac{48}{12}+\frac{7}{12}=4\frac{7}{12}$$

The final answer is a *mixed number* that contains both a whole number and a fraction. Mixed numbers can be added by keeping the whole numbers and the fractions separate, and subtracted by 'adding back' to give a whole number. For example:

$$2\frac{3}{4}+1\frac{1}{8}=2+1+\frac{6}{8}+\frac{1}{8}=3\frac{7}{8}$$

$$5\frac{3}{4}-1\frac{1}{8}=\frac{7}{8}+3+\frac{3}{4}\text{ (adding back to 2, then 5, then }5\frac{3}{4}\text{)}$$

$$3\frac{7}{8}+\frac{6}{8}=3\frac{13}{8}=3+\frac{8}{8}+\frac{5}{8}=4\frac{5}{8}$$

Mixed numbers have to be converted into improper fractions before multiplying and dividing. For example:

$$1\frac{3}{8}\times1\frac{3}{4}=\frac{11}{8}\times\frac{7}{4}=\frac{77}{32}=\frac{64}{32}+\frac{13}{32}=2\frac{13}{32}$$

Ratio and proportion

Ratios are similar to fractions. They show how a whole is divided into parts. For example:

Divide 60 in the ratio 1:3

Method:

Step 1: work out the number of parts in the whole, in this case: $1 + 3 = 4$ (four quarters).
Step 2: work out the proportional parts (the fractions); these are $\frac{1}{4}$ and $\frac{3}{4}$.
Step 3: multiply the whole (60) by the proportional parts:
$\frac{1}{4} \times 60 = 15$ $(60 \div 4 = 15)$
$\frac{3}{4} \times 60 = 45$ $(60 \div 4 \times 3 = 45)$.
The proportional parts when added together give the whole: $15 + 45 = 60$.

Ratios can be simplified in a similar way to fractions by cancelling both sides by a common factor (by 2, by 3, etc). For example:

> The ratio of boys to girls in a science class of 28 is 16:12. Express this ratio in its simplest terms:
> 16:12 = 8:6 = 4:3, ie there are 4 boys for every 3 girls.

Decimals (decimal fractions)

Fractions have an equivalent decimal as shown in the examples below. The more common decimals are worth remembering, for example:

0.25 = nought point two five = one-quarter
0.5 = nought point five = one-half
0.75 = nought point seven five = three-quarters
0.1 = nought point one = one-tenth
0.2 = nought point two = one-fifth
0.125 = nought point one two five = one-eighth
0.375 = nought point three seven five = three-eighths
0.01 = nought point nought one = one hundredth
0.001 = nought point nought nought one = one-thousandth
0.005 = nought point nought nought five = five-thousandths

Addition and subtraction

The decimal points should be aligned; eg 0.68 + 0.062 + 0.20; re-write as:

0.680
0.062
0.200+
0.942

Multiplication

To multiply by multiples (powers) of 10 the decimal point is moved to the right by the respective number of zeros. For example:

0.75 × 10 = 7.5
0.75 × 100 = 75
0.75 × 1000 = 750

To multiply decimals by numbers other than 10 you ignore the decimal point and then add it back in using the following rule: *number of decimal places in the question = number of decimal places in the answer.* For example:

8 × 10.24 ignore the decimal point:
8 × 1024 = 8 × 1000 + 8 × 20 + 8 × 4 = 8000 + 160 + 32 = 8192
number of decimal places = 2, ie 8192 becomes 81.92

Division

Division of decimal numbers is the reverse of the multiplication case, ie you move the decimal point to the left. For example:

25.75 ÷ 10 = 2.575
25.75 ÷ 100 = 0.2575
25.75 ÷ 1000 = 0.02575

Division of decimal numbers can be carried out in the same way as with whole numbers, keeping the decimal point in the same vertical column. For example:

$$75.25 \div 5 \qquad \begin{array}{r} 15.05 \\ \hline 7^{2}5.2^{2}5 \end{array} \qquad \text{or } 75.25 \div 5 = 75 \div 5 + 0.25 \div 5$$

In practice it is often quicker to use powers of 10 to facilitate any division involving decimal numbers. For example:

75.25 ÷ 5 = 150.5 ÷ 10 = 15.05

To divide by a decimal number the decimal must be converted to a whole number as a first step. For example:

> 18 ÷ 0.15 is re-written as 1800 ÷ 15 by multiplying both numbers by 100 to remove the decimal point from the 0.15; then 1800 ÷ 15 = 120.

In the following example the decimal is not multiplied by a power of 10 but by the smallest number that will produce a whole number to divide by (ie × 4):

70.5 ÷ 0.25 = 70.5 × 4 ÷ 0.25 × 4 = 282 ÷ 1.0 = 282

Note that dividing by 1/4 is the same as multiplying by 4 (turn the fraction upside-down and multiply), ie:

÷ 0.25 = ÷ 1/4 = × 4
÷ 0.5 = ÷ 1/2 = × 2
÷ 0.1 = ÷ 1/10 = × 10
÷ 0.2 = ÷ 2/10 = ÷ 1/5 = × 5
÷ 0.01 = ÷ 1/100 = × 100
÷ 0.005 = ÷ 5/1000 = × 1000/5 = × 200

The above examples also show how decimals can be converted to fractions with denominators of 10, 100 or 1000. For example:

0.2 = two-tenths = 2/10 = 1/5
0.25 = twenty-five hundredths= 25/100 = 5/20 =1/4
0.005 = five-thousands = 5/1000 = 1/200

Percent and percentage change

Percent

A percent (%) is a special case of a fraction where the denominator is always 100. For example:

$$60\% = \frac{60}{100} = \frac{6}{10} = \frac{3}{5} \quad 75\% = \frac{75}{100} = \frac{15}{20} = \frac{3}{4}$$

A percent can be expressed as a decimal by dividing the numerator by 100, ie by moving the decimal point of the numerator two places to the left. For example:

$$60\% = \frac{60.0}{100} = 0.6 \qquad 75\% = \frac{75.0}{100} = 0.75$$

To work out a percentage figure you multiply by the percent expressed either as a fraction or as a decimal. For example:

Find 25% of 120

$$25\% = 25 \div 100 = 0.25; 0.25 \times 120 = 2.5 \times 12 = 30, \text{ or}$$

$$25\% = \frac{25}{100} = \frac{1}{4}; \qquad \frac{1}{4} \times 120 = 120 \div 4 = 30$$

In the above example, the fraction method of working out the percentage was easier than the decimal method but in some cases the reverse is true.

You should be familiar with the following fractions and their equivalent decimal and percent values:

$$\frac{1}{10} = 0.1 = 10\%$$

$$\frac{1}{4} = 0.25 = 25\%$$

$$\frac{1}{3} = 0.33 = 33.3\%$$

$$\frac{1}{2} = 0.5 = 50\%$$

$$\frac{2}{3} = 0.67 = 66.7\%$$

$$\frac{3}{4} = 0.75 = 75\%$$

$$\frac{1}{8} = 0.125 = 12.5\%$$

$$\frac{3}{8} = 0.375 = 37.5\%$$

To convert a less obvious fraction to a decimal or a percent you need to express the denominator as a factor of 100:

$$\frac{9}{25} = \frac{9 \times 4}{25 \times 4} = \frac{36}{100} = 0.36 = 36\%$$

$$\frac{11}{20} = \frac{11 \times 5}{20 \times 5} = \frac{55}{100} = 0.55 = 55\%$$

Percentage change (increase or decrease)

$$\text{Percentage change} = \frac{\text{change in value}}{\text{original value}} \times 100\%$$

For example:

A school bus accelerates from 40 mph to 60 mph. What is the percentage increase in speed?

$$\text{Percentage increase} = \frac{60 - 40}{40} \times 100\%$$

$$= \frac{20}{40} \times 100\% = 0.5 \times 100\% = 50\% \text{ increase}$$

A school mini-bus brakes from 60 mph to 40 mph. What is the percentage decrease in speed?

$$\text{Percentage change} = \frac{60 - 40}{60} \times 100\%$$

$$= \frac{20}{60} \times 100\% = \frac{1}{3} \times 100\% = 33.3\% \text{ decrease}$$

Always use the original/initial value as the denominator when calculating a percentage change.

Time

Candidates should be familiar with both the 12-hour clock and the 24-hour clock, which starts and finishes at midnight, ie midnight = 0000 hours or 2400 hours (twenty-four hundred hours); noon (midday) = 1200 hrs (twelve hundred hours).

Times can be converted from the 12-hour clock to the 24-hour clock by re-writing the time as a four digit number and adding 12 hours to all pm times. For example:

9.30 am = 0930 hrs (O nine-thirty hours)
3 pm = 3 + 12 hrs = 1500 hrs (fifteen hundred hours)
10.55 pm = 10.55 + 12 hrs = 2255 (twenty-two fifty-five hours)

Always use this four digit format when responding to QTS questions; there is no need to include the word 'hours' in your answers.

Fractional parts of an hour are converted to minutes by multiplying the fraction (or its decimal) by 60 minutes:

$\frac{1}{4}$ hr = 0.25 hr = 0.25 × 60 = 15 min
$^{1}/_{10}$ hr = 0.1 hr = 0.1 × 60 = 6 min

You can add or subtract times as follows:

1445 hrs + 1 hr 50 min = 1445 + 2 hr – 10 min = 1635 hrs
2235 hrs – 55 min = 2235 hrs – 1 hr + 5 min = 2140 hrs
3.5 hr + 10 min = 3 hr + 30 min + 10 min = 3 hr 40 min.
4 hr ÷ 6 = 4 × 60 ÷ 6 = 4 × 10 = 40 min

Money

Always use the decimal point format when answering QTS questions that involve money; the currency sign is optional. For example:

£3.45 + 65 pence = 345p + 65p = 410p = £4.10, or
£3.45 + 65 pence = £3.45 + £0.65 = £4.10

There is no need to include a letter 'p' after the pence.

Calculations that involve different currencies require that you either multiply or divide by the exchange rate. For example:

If £1 = 2.25 Swiss francs (CHF), how many Swiss francs are there in £60?

£1 = 2.25 Swiss francs (CHF) then £60 = 60 × 2.25 CHF
= 60 × 2 + 60 × 1/4
= 120 + 15 = 135 CHF

If £1 = 2.25 Swiss francs (CHF), how many pounds are there in 90 CHF?

> 90 CHF = 90 ÷ 2.25 pounds
> multiply 2.25 × 4 (removes the decimal point) to give 9
> then multiply 90 × 4 to match, ie:
> 90 ÷ 2.25 = 90 × 4 ÷ 9 = 10 × 4 = £40
> (check: 40 × 2.25 = 80 + 10 = 90)

Mental arithmetic questions

Introduction

The first section of the test is an aural mental arithmetic test heard through the computer's headphones. Each question is read out twice with no pause in between. You will then be given 18 seconds in which to enter your answer using the keyboard before the next question is read out. You are not allowed to use a calculator but you will have access to a pen and paper to jot down the calculation. The following points are worth noting:

- Write down any numbers and attempt the question straight away without waiting for it to be read out a second time. There is less time to spare than you might think.
- Do not continue with any question beyond the allotted time. Leave it and move on to the next question. Do not pursue any answer at the expense of missing the next question.
- Most questions will involve more than one arithmetic process (eg multiplication followed by division or cancelling).
- There are no right and wrong methods. Your answers will be marked by a computer. This book contains tips and exemplar methods but use any arithmetic techniques that work for you.

- The context of the question is irrelevant to the maths involved. You simply apply the four arithmetic operations of addition, subtraction, multiplication and division to fractions, decimals, percentages, time, money and measurements.

There now follows a mental arithmetic exemplar test and five similar tests with answers at the end of the book. You will need a pen and paper but not a calculator. You can simulate the actual test more accurately by having someone read the questions out aloud for you or by recording the questions and then playing them back.

Exemplar test with answers

1. In a school of one hundred and eighty-five pupils, one-fifth take free school meals. How many take free school meals?

   $185 \div 5 = 200 \div 5 - 15 \div 5 = 40 - 3 =$ **37**

2. A school library contains two hundred and fifty-two books. If the ratio of non-fiction to fiction books is five to one, how many fiction books are there?

   $5n + n = 252$; $6n = 252$; $n = 240 \div 6 + 12 \div 6 = 40 + 2 =$ **42**

3. If one gallon is equivalent to four point five litres, how many gallons are there in three litres? Give your answer as a fraction.

   1 gal = 4.5 l; so 1 l = $1 \div 4.5$; 3 l = $3 \div 4.5 = 30 \div 45 =$ **2/3**

4. A school can buy twenty books at seven pounds and fifty pence each or borrow the books from a library service at a cost of fifty pounds. How much money will be saved by borrowing the books?

   $20 \times £7.50 = 2 \times £75 = £150$; $£150 - 50 =$ **£100**

5. A school audio CD costs six pounds plus VAT. If VAT is charged at seventeen and one-half percent how much does the CD cost to the nearest penny?

$17.5\% = 17.5$ p per pound (100p); $17.5 \times 6 = 18 \times 6 - 0.5 \times 6$
$= 60 + 48 - 3 = 60 + 45 = £1.05$; $+ £6 =$ **£7.05**

6. Three hundred and twenty pupils sat GCSE English. If sixty-five percent of the pupils achieved grade C or below, how many achieved grade B or above?

$100\% - 65\% = 35\%$; $35\% \times 320 = 0.35 \times 320 = 3.5 \times 32$
$= 3 \times 32 + 0.5 \times 32 = 96 + 16 =$ **112**

7. What is sixty-two and one-half percent as a fraction?

$62.5\% = 62.5/100 = 125/200 = 25/40 =$ **5/8**

8. A school coach arrived at the Tate Gallery at thirteen hundred hours. The journey took one hour and thirty-five minutes excluding a fifteen minute break. What time was it when the coach set out?

Total time taken = 1 hrs 35 min + 15 min = 1 hr 50 min
1300 hrs – 1 hr 50 min = 1300 hrs – 2 hr + 10 min = **1110**

9. In a school run a pupil completed three miles around a four hundred metre track. How many laps of the track were completed if one mile is equivalent to one point six kilometres?

3 miles = $3 \times 1.6 = 4.8$ km
4.8 km $\times$ 1000 m/km = 48×100 m = 4800 m
$4800 \div 400 = 48 \div 4 =$ **12**

10. A ski trip to Switzerland costs six hundred pounds and requires a deposit of thirty percent. What is the deposit in Swiss francs if one pound is equivalent to two Swiss francs?

$£600 \times 30\% = £600 \times 0.3 = £60 \times 3 = £180$
$£180 \times 2$ Swiss francs per pound = **360**

11. A school playground measures sixteen metres by twelve point five metres. What is its area in metres squared?

$16 \times 12.5 = 16 \times 10 + 16 \times 2.5 = 160 + 40 = \mathbf{200}$
($x2.5 = 1/4$ of $x10$; or $16 \times 2.5 = 16 \times 2 + 0.5 \times 2$; or $16 \times 5 \div 2$)

12. An 11–18 comprehensive school has fifteen hundred pupils on roll, including one hundred and eighty A-level students. What percentage of the pupils on roll are A-level students?

$180 \div 1500 \times 100\% = 180 \div 15 = 150 \div 15 + 30 \div 15 = \mathbf{12}$

Mental Arithmetic Test 1
(time allowed = 10 minutes)

1. In a school of three hundred and twenty-four pupils, one-sixth take free school meals. How many take free school meals?

2. A school library contains one hundred and fifty-six books. If the number of non-fiction books is twice the number of fiction books, how many non-fiction books are there?

3. If one gallon is equivalent to four point five litres, how many gallons are there in one litre? Give your answer as a fraction.

4. A school can buy ten books at nine pounds and ninety-five pence each or borrow the books from a library service at a cost of forty pounds. How much money will be saved by borrowing the books?

5. A school audio CD costs five pounds plus VAT. If VAT is charged at seventeen and one-half percent, how much does the CD cost to the nearest penny?

6. Two hundred and forty pupils sat GCSE English. If forty-five percent of the pupils achieved grade D or below, how many achieved grade C or above?

7. A school coach arrives at the Tate Gallery at twelve hundred hours. The journey took two hours and twenty-five minutes excluding a fifteen minute break. At what time did the coach set out?

8. In a school run a pupil completed five miles around a four hundred metre track. How many laps of the track were completed if one mile is equivalent to one point six kilometres?

9. A ski trip to Switzerland cost seven hundred and fifty pounds with a twenty percent deposit. What is the deposit in Swiss francs if one pound is equivalent to two Swiss francs?

10. What is thirty-seven and one-half percent as a fraction?

11. A school playground measures twelve metres by thirteen point five metres. What is its area in metres squared?

12. An 11–18 comprehensive school has fifteen hundred and fifty pupils on roll including three hundred and ten A-level students. What percentage of the pupils on roll are A-level students?

Mental Arithmetic Test 2
(time allowed = 10 minutes)

1. School dinners cost one pound and eighty-five pence each. A pupil pays in advance for a week's dinners. What is the correct change in pence out of a ten pound note?

2. A school with nine hundred and fifty places has an occupancy rate of ninety-four percent. How many more pupils could it take?

3. A school has two hundred and ninety boys and three hundred and ten girls. How many girls would you expect

there to be in a representative sample of one hundred and twenty pupils?

4. An exam finished at twelve twenty-five hours having lasted one and three-quarter hours. At what time did the exam start?

5. In a sponsored run a pupil completed twenty laps around a four hundred metre track. How many miles did he complete if one kilometre is equal to five-eighths of a mile?

6. In a secondary school with nine hundred pupils, four out of every five pupils own a mobile phone. How many pupils do not own a mobile phone?

7. A sponsored walk by five hundred pupils raised six thousand, nine hundred and fifty pounds for charity. What was the average amount raised per pupil?

8. A school trip to the Tate Gallery took two hours and fifteen minutes by coach, travelling at an average speed of forty miles per hour. How far away was the gallery?

9. A pupil gained thirty marks out of fifty in one Maths test and sixteen marks out of twenty-five in a second Maths test. What was the average percentage for the two tests assuming they were weighted equally?

10. What is sixty-two and one-half percent as a decimal fraction to one decimal place?

11. A school skiing trip costs seven hundred and twenty pounds per pupil with a fifteen percent deposit. How much is the deposit in Euros if there are one point two-five Euros to the pound?

12. Teachers at a school have four hours and twelve minutes contact time per day. What is the contact time per week?

Mental Arithmetic Test 3 (time allowed = 10 minutes)

1. A pupil aged eleven years and four months has a reading age eighteen months below his actual age. What is his reading age?

2. A geography school trip costs seventy pounds and the deposit is fourteen pounds. What percentage of the cost is the deposit?

3. Out of one hundred and forty-four pupils who sat GCSE English Literature, ninety achieved grades A to C. What fraction achieved grades A to C?

4. In a primary school, five percent of half-day sessions were missed through absence. If there were three hundred and eighty half-day sessions, how many were missed through absence?

5. How many school books at eight pounds and seventy-five pence each can be bought on a budget of one hundred pounds?

6. The highest mark in a Maths test was forty-six correct answers out of fifty questions and the lowest mark was twenty-five correct answers out of fifty questions. What is the difference between the highest and lowest marks in percentage points?

7. A ski trip to Switzerland costs eight hundred pounds per pupil and requires a twenty-five percent deposit. What is the deposit in Swiss francs if one hundred pounds buys two hundred and five Swiss francs?

8. What is four-fifths as a percentage?

9. A fence is to be erected around a school playing field. The field is rectangular in shape and measures one hundred and

twenty metres by ninety metres. What length of fence will be needed?

10. What is two point five percent as a fraction in its lowest terms?

11. The teacher to pupil ratio on a school trip is not to be less than one to fifteen. If there are one hundred and seventy-two pupils going on the trip, how many teachers will be required?

12. A school day starts at eight-fifty am and finishes at three-thirty pm. Breaks total one hour and fifteen minutes. What is the maximum number of half-hour lessons possible per day?

Mental Arithmetic Test 4 9
(time allowed = 10 minutes)

1. At the start of a school day the library contains twelve thousand books. By the end of the day one hundred and twenty-three books have been loaned out and fifty-seven books have been returned. How many books are there in the library at the end of the day?

2. In a class of twenty-five pupils, forty percent are girls. How many boys are there in the class?

3. GCSE pupils take a Double Science or Single Science award. If Double Science is seven times more popular than the Single Science, what fraction of the pupils take Single Science?

4. The cost of a school ski trip was six hundred and sixty pounds per pupil last year. This year the cost will increase by three percent. What will be the cost per pupil this year? Give your answer to the nearest pound.

5. What is zero point four five as a fraction?

6. In a year group, seven out of every ten pupils achieved Key Stage 2. What percentage of the pupils failed to achieve Key Stage 2?

7. How many pieces of card measuring thirty centimetres by twenty centimetres can be cut from a sheet measuring one point five metres by one point one metres?

8. A pupil is one point six metres tall. If there are two point five centimetres to the inch, how tall is the pupil in inches?

9. School lessons start at a quarter past nine. There are ten lessons per day lasting thirty minutes each and breaks that total ninety minutes. What time does the school day finish?

10. A school minibus averages thirty miles per gallon. A teacher fills the tank with forty-five litres of fuel. How far can the minibus travel if one gallon is equivalent to four and one-half litres?

11. A test has a pass mark of seventy percent. If there are thirty-five questions, what is the minimum number of correct answers necessary to pass the test?

12. In a school of one hundred and ninety-two pupils, seven-twelfths are boys. How many girls are there?

Mental Arithmetic Test 5 (time allowed = 10 minutes)

1. Four hundred and twenty-four pupils in a year group sit GCSE Maths. If seventy-nine pupils failed to achieve grade C or above, how many pupils did achieve grade C or above?

2. The cost of a school trip to France was four hundred and thirty pounds last year. This year the trip will cost eleven percent more. What will be the cost of the trip this year?

3. GCSE pupils take Triple, Double or Single Science. If three-quarters take the Double Science and one-sixth take Single Science, how many take Triple Science?

4. A school charges six pence per A4 page for photocopying, thirty pence for binding and twenty-five pence for a clear cover. What is the cost of two one-hundred page books bound with clear front and back covers?

5. What is twenty-two point five percent as a decimal fraction?

6. The average weight of a class of eleven-year-old pupils is forty kilograms. What is this in pounds if one kilogram is equivalent to two point two pounds?

7. A school teacher hires a minibus at fifty pounds per day plus the cost of the petrol used. The minibus uses one litre of fuel for every ten kilometres travelled. If fuel costs one pound and fifty pence per litre, how much would it cost for a one-day round trip of two hundred kilometres?

8. The pass mark in a class test is sixty percent. If there are forty-two questions, how many must be answered correctly to pass?

9. What is zero point zero five multiplied by one thousand?

10. A school trip requires three forty-seater coaches to hold the pupils and teachers. Two of the coaches are full and the third is three-quarters full. How many teachers went on the trip if there was one teacher for every nine pupils?

11. A school wildlife pond is four metres in diameter. What is the diameter of the pond on a fifty to one scale drawing?

12. A school day ends at five past three. There are two lessons in the afternoon each lasting fifty minutes with a ten minute break in between. At what time does the first afternoon lesson begin?

2

General arithmetic

Maths audit 2

For the general arithmetic questions you need to know the following.

Decimal numbers

- How to round a decimal to the nearest whole number.
- How to shorten a decimal number to a given number of decimal places.

Measurement

- How to convert units of weight, length and volume in the metric system.
- How to work out the areas of basic shapes and borders.
- How to work out perimeters.
- How to read scales on maps.

Averages

- How to work out the arithmetic mean, median and modal value (mode).
- How to work out weighted averages.

Algebra

- How to work out arithmetic problems that contain brackets.
- How to solve problems that contain two or more arithmetic signs using the correct sequence of operations ('BIDMAS').
- How to work out simple formulae.

Decimal numbers

Sometimes the numbers you obtain from a calculation give a higher level of accuracy than is required for a sensible answer. For example:

$3.75 \times 4.29 = 16.0875$

To *correct* the answer to a given number of decimal places you shorten the number of decimal places (dp) so that is has 3, 2 or 1 decimal places.

If the *number to the right* of the decimal place you are rounding to is *5 or above*, then you increase the number in the decimal place by 1; if it is less than 5 it remains the same. Examples are:

16.0875 to 3 dp =16.088
16.0875 to 2 dp =16.09
16.0875 to 1 dp =16.1
16.0875 to 0 dp = 16
0.069827 = 0.0698 to 4 dp (2 is less than 5, so the 8 remains the same)

0.069827 = 0.070 to 3 dp (the 8 is more than 5, so 9 becomes 10)

Note that rounding a decimal to the nearest whole number is the same as rounding to 0 decimal places. Examples are:

22.49 to the nearest whole number is 22.0 or 22 (round down)
22.50 to the nearest whole number is 23.0 or 23 (round up)

The metric system of measurement (SI units)

The most important metric measurements are weight, length and volume. SI units (international system) are in most cases the same as metric units, all being based on units of 10.

Weight

The basic unit of weight is the gram (g). All metric weights are based on this. There are three weights you are likely to encounter:

Name	Symbol
kilogram	kg
gram	g
milligram	mg

1 kg = 1000 g; 1 g = 1000 mg

Length

The basic unit of length is the metre (m). All metric lengths are based on this. There are four lengths you may encounter:

Name	Symbol
kilometre	km
metre	m
centimetre	cm
millimetre	mm

1 km = 1000 m; 1 m = 100 cm; 1 cm = 10 mm

Volume of liquids and gases (capacity)

Quantities of liquids and gases are measured in litres (l) and millilitres (ml) where 1 l = 1000 ml. You may also come across:

decilitre (dl) = one-tenth of a litre = 100 ml
centilitre (cl) = one-hundredth of a litre = 10 ml
cubic centimetre (cc or cm^3) = one-thousandth of a litre = 1 ml

Adding and subtracting metric units

When working out sums with metric units it is important that all the numbers have the same units. For example:

add 5 cm to 2 m, ie:
2 m + 5 cm = 2 m + 0.05 m = 2.05 m
1 g + 25 mg = 1 g + 0.025 g = 1.025 g
0.6 g – 500 mg = 600 mg – 500 mg = 100 mg or
0.6g – 500 mg = 0.6g – 0.5g = 0.1g

Areas, borders, perimeters and volumes

Areas

The metric units of area are square metre (m^2), square centimetre (cm^2) and square millimetre (mm^2).

Area of a square of side length a = a × a = a^2.

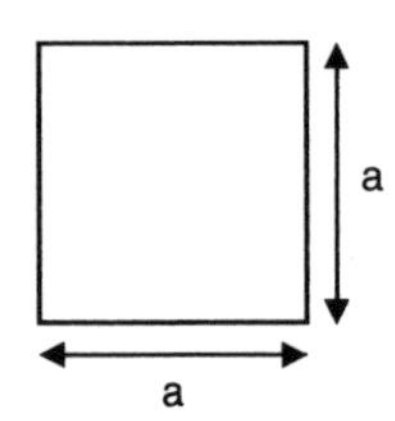

Area = of a rectangle = length (l) × breadth (b) = l × b .

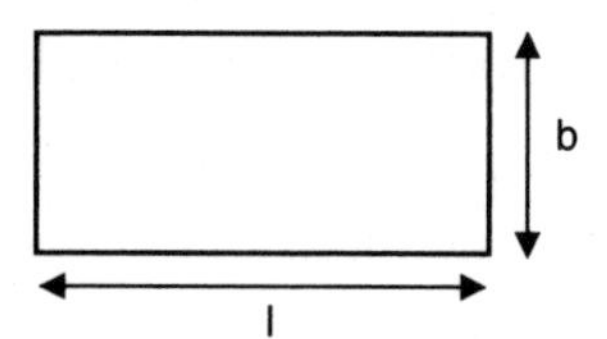

The area of any triangle is found by multiplying half the base by the vertical height.

Area = ½ base × vertical height = ½ bh

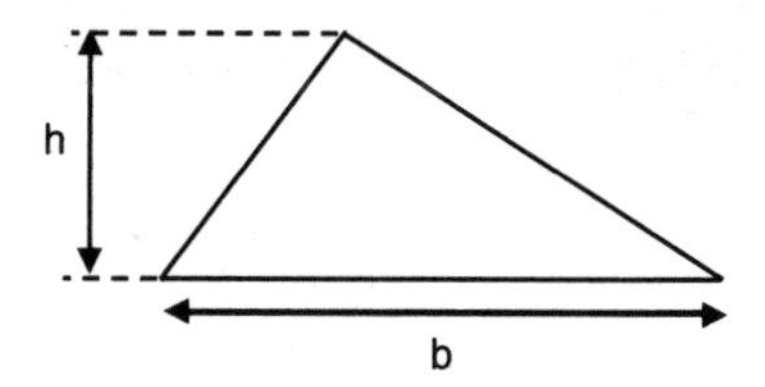

Area of a circle of radius r = πr^2 (pi r squared). The diameter is twice as long as the radius, ie D = 2r and r = ½ D. Substituting ½ D for r in πr^2 gives:

Area = $\pi (\frac{1}{2} D)^2 = \pi \times \frac{1}{2} D \times \frac{1}{2} D = \pi \frac{1}{4} D^2 = \pi \times \frac{D^2}{4}$

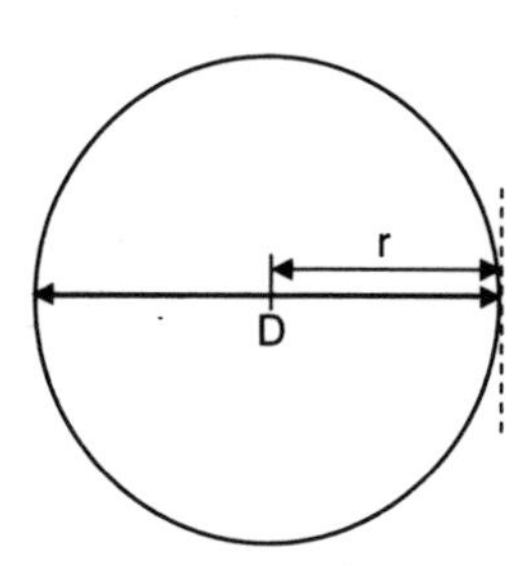

π = 3.142 (to 3 dp) or roughly $\frac{22}{7}$

Borders

The area of any border is given by the area of the outside shape minus area of the inside shape. For example:

Area of border = area outer rectangle – area inner rectangle
$= 12 \times 6 - 8 \times 4$
$= 72 - 32 = 40\ \text{cm}^2$

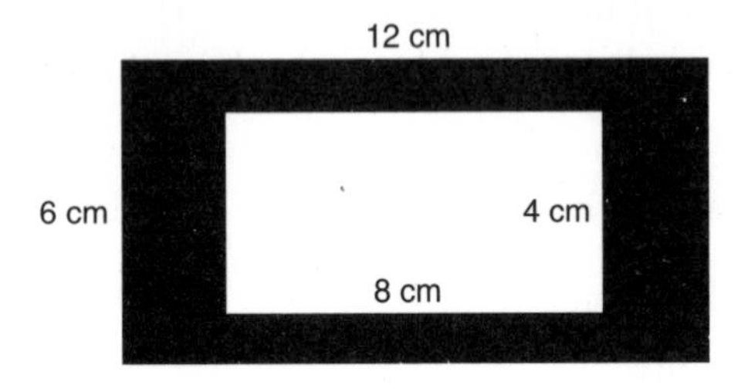

Perimeters

The perimeter of any shape is the distance all the way around the outside of the shape. Examples are:

Perimeter of a square = 4 × length of side

Perimeter of a rectangle = 2 × length × breadth

Perimeter of a circle = circumference: $C = 2\pi r = \pi D$

Volumes of solids

Volume is a measure of the space taken up by a three-dimensional object. It is measured in units cubed (units^3) and the standard units of volume are the cubic metre (m^3), cubic centimetre (cm^3) and the cubic millimetre (mm^3).

The most common solids have a prism shape, which means they have the same cross-section throughout their length.

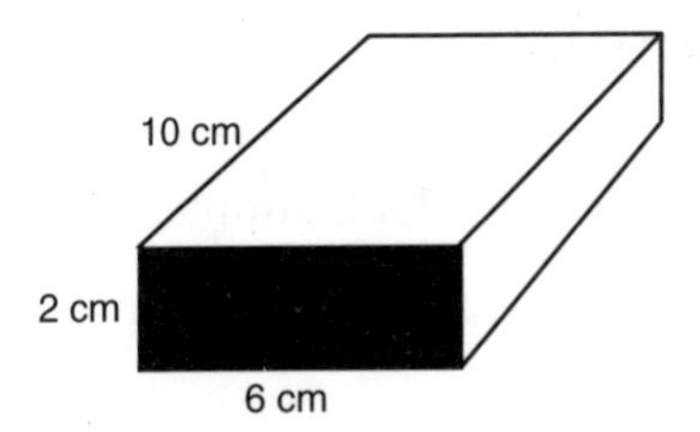

Volume = area of front face × length = 2 × 6 × 10 = 120 cm^3

Scales

These are used when something very large is drawn in reduced form. Typical examples are maps and scale drawings of houses (blueprints). Scales are usually given in the form of a ratio of length (or distance) on the scale drawing to a length (or distance) of the real thing. Scales can vary enormously from, for example, one-sixth scale (eg house floor plans) to one fifty-thousandth scale (eg for maps).

Scales can be shown as either a fraction, eg ¼ or as a proportion, eg 1:4 (one to four) meaning that one unit of length on the drawing represents four units of length on the real thing. A map scale given as $^1/_{50000}$ or 1:50000 means that one unit of length on the map is equivalent to 50000 units on the ground, ie 1 cm on the map = 50000 cm on the ground = 500 m = 0.5 km. So 1 cm on the map equals 0.5 km on the ground (a '2 cm to 1 km' map). The most popular map scale is 1:25000 scale, which is the same as 1 cm : 0.25 km (a '4 cm to 1 km' map). Another way to show a map scale is to use a graphic, as shown below. Here the scale will remain true even if the size of the map is changed by photocopying.

0 1 2 3 4
km

Aspects of algebra

There are arithmetic rules for positively signed and negatively signed numbers. The following examples explain the correct procedures for combining signs:

$12 - 3 = 9$
$-12 - 3 = -15$
$-12 + 3 = -9$
$-12 \times 3 = -36$
$-12 \times -3 = 36$
$12 \div -3 = -4$
$-12 \div 3 = -4$
$-12 \div -3 = 4$
$-12 \times -3 \times -2 = -72$
$-12 \times -3 \times -2 \times -2 = 144$

Multiplication signs are omitted if brackets are used:
$(-12)(-3)(-2) = -72$, ie not $(-12) \times (-3) \times (-2) = -72$

BIDMAS

The order of working out problems is:

B = Brackets;
I = Indices;
D = Division;
M = Multiplication;
A = Addition;
S = Subtraction

There is a definite order in which to work out a sum containing more than one arithmetic sign. The rule is: brackets first followed by indices (powers) then division or multiplication and finally addition or subtraction. For example:

$(9 + 11) \times 2 = 20 \times 2 = 40$
without brackets this calculation becomes:
$9 + 11 \times 2 = 9 + 22 = 31$

Letters can be used in place of numbers to describe the 'general case' of something. The letters x and y are the most common letters employed in algebra. x and y are known as variables because their values can be varied; numbers have fixed values and are constants.

The first skill of algebra involves substituting numbers for the letters. For example:

If $x = 5$ and $y = 7$ find:
$x + y$ $(5 + 7 = 12)$
$2x - y$ $(10 - 7 = 3)$
$x^2 + 3y - 3$ $(25 + 21 - 3 = 43)$ (x^2 = x squared = $x \times x$)

If $x = 2$ and $y = -2$, find:
$x + y$ $(2 + (-2) = 0)$
$x - y$ $(2 - (-2) = 2 + 2 = 4)$
xy (ie x times y) $(2 \times (-2) = -4)$

Another skill is removing brackets, also known as 'expanding' an expression. A 'term' outside a bracket multiplies each of the terms inside the bracket, moving from left to right:

$3(y - 5z)$ = 3 times y plus 3 times $-5z$ = $3y - 15z$
Similarly: $-2y(6 - 3x + z) = -12y + 6xy - 2yz$

A further skill is that of rearranging a formula (an equation with two or more variables). Take the following formula for example:

$x = y + z$

To make y the subject of the formula, subtract z from both sides of the equation to $x - z = y + z - z$, to give:

$x - z = y$ ie $y = x - z$

To make z the subject of the formula, subtract y from both sides of the equation to *leave z on its own*:

$x - y = y + z - y$, gives:
$x - y = z$ ie $z = x - y$

Example: Find x if $3x + y = z$ (ie x is the subject of the formula)
Method:
Step 1: subtract y from both sides
$3x + y - y = z - y$
$3x = z - y$
Step 2: divide both sides of the equation by 3

$$\frac{3x}{3} = \frac{z - y}{3} \text{ so } x = \frac{z - y}{3}$$

Rearranging linear equations

Linear equations have letters with a power of one – there are no squared terms. Examples of linear equations can be found in mathematics, science and everyday life. Typical examples are:

temperature conversion;
speed, distance and time;
ratio and proportion;
maps and scales;
VAT and income tax; and
electrical power.

Examples of linear equations and algebraic manipulation are:

calculate distance travelled (D) from speed (S) and time (T):
$D = ST$ (and $T = D \div S$; $S = D \div T$)

calculate power in Watts (W) from volts (V) and amps (A):
$W = VA$ (and $V = W \div A$; $A = W \div V$)

The following formula is more difficult to rearrange because it requires more than one step. In the test you will only be required to insert values into a formula to arrive at the answer. However, your ability to find solutions to problems will increase if you can move letters and numbers around easily from one side of an equation to the other.

To convert temperature from Fahrenheit to Celsius:

rearrange $F = \frac{9}{5}C + 32$ to leave C on its own:

i) subtract 32 from both sides to give $F - 32 = \frac{9}{5}C + 0$

ii) now multiply both sides by $\frac{5}{9}$ to give $\frac{5}{9}(F - 32) = \frac{5}{9} \times \frac{9}{5}C$

So $\frac{5}{9}(F - 32) = 1 \times C$, ie $C = \frac{5}{9}(F - 32)$ to convert Celcius to Fahrenheit: rearrange $C = \frac{5}{9}(F - 32)$ to leave F on its own:

i) multiply both sides by $\frac{9}{5}$ to give $\frac{9}{5}C = F - 32$ in a single step

ii) add 32 to both sides to give $\frac{9}{5}C + 32 = F$, ie $F = \frac{9}{5}C + 32$;

(also $F = 1.8C + 32$ or $F = (C + 40) \times 1.8 - 40$)

Trends

You may be asked to spot a trend in a data series, typically an increase or decrease in a value with time; for example, school admissions over several years. In an *arithmetic series* there is a *common difference* between the numbers that enables you to predict the next number in the series. Examples include:

200 400 600 800 ___? (common difference = 200)
300 350 400 450 ___? (common difference = 50)
65 59 53 47 41 ___? (common difference = 6)
7.8 6.1 4.4 2.7 _? (common difference = 1.7)

In another type of series the difference between consecutive numbers increases (or decreases) with each change, for example:

1	2	4	7	11	16	22	_?
+1	+2	+3	+4	+5	+6	+7	

In a *geometric series* the *ratio* of consecutive number is constant, for example, the numbers double or half in value:

1 2 4 8 16 32 64 128 256 512 ___?
(common ratio = 2)
96 48 24 12 6 _? (common ratio = 0.50)
20000 4000 800 160 32 _? (common ratio = 0.2)

Averages

You might have a group of numbers (a data set) and wish to find a single number that best represents the group, ie a central value. The most common method is to calculate the arithmetic mean.

Mean

Add all the numbers together then divide the total by the number of numbers. For example:

What is the mean height of the following group of pupils: 1.55 m, 1.62 m, 1.57 m, 1.65 m and 1.51m?

The mean is the sum total of the heights divided by five:

$$\frac{1.55 + 1.62 + 1.57 + 1.65 + 1.51}{5} = 7.9 \text{ m} \div 5 = 1.58 \text{ m}$$

Alternatives to the mean are the median and mode.

Median

The median is the middle number in a group of numbers that have been placed in numerical order, from smallest to the largest. From the previous example:

1st	2nd	3rd	4th	5th
1.51	1.55	1.57	1.62	1.65

The median is given by the middle value, which in this case is the third number, ie 1.57 m.

Here is another example. What is the median average of the following numbers?

4.3 10 3 7.5 5 9 6.7 5

Step 1: rearrange in ascending order, repeating any numbers where necessary:

3 4.3 5 5 6.7 7.5 9 10

There is an even number of numbers in this group and, therefore, no 'middle value' as such.

Step 2: to find the 'middle value' you work out the mean of the two middle numbers:

5 + 6.7 = 11.7 ÷ 2 = 5.85 = median of the group.

To locate the middle position of a large group of numbers (n), add 1 and divide by 2, ie (n + 1) ÷ 2. For example:

You have 51 numbers. The middle position (median) is found by adding 1 and dividing by 2: (51 +1) ÷ 2 = 26th number.
You have 50 numbers. The middle position is found by adding 1 and dividing by 2: (50 +1) ÷ 2 = 25.5 so you have to average the 25th and 26th numbers to find the median.

Mode

The mode is the value that occurs most often.

For example in this group of numbers – 3 4 7 3 4 5 3 9 8 6 3 – the mode (modal value) is 3 because it occurs most frequently – four times. If two values are equally popular then the group is said to be 'bi-modal'. For example, in the group 5 5 7 8 3 7 4 1 2, the modal values are 5 and 7.

If more than two numbers occur equally most frequently in a group then the mode would not be used as a way of expressing the average value.

Range

The range measures the spread of the data, ie the maximum value minus the minimum value. For example:

5 5 7 8 3 7 4 1 2 – range = 8 – 1 = 7

Weighted average

In a weighted average test, some scores count more than others towards the overall result. Weighted averages are used in coursework and in university degree classification. Examples of degree course weighting are:

1:3:5 first year = 1/9; second year = 3/9; final year = 5/9
1:3 second year = 25%; final year = 75%
1:2 second year = 0.33; final year = 0.67

The weighted average is calculated as follows:

i) convert each mark or score to its percentage (eg 16 correct answers out of 20 marks = 80%);
ii) multiply each percentage mark by its weight (expressed as either a fraction, percentage or decimal);
iii) sum the results, giving your answer a percentage.

The following equations show you how to work out the weighted average of the three examples given above:

1:3:5 Overall mark = (1 × Yr1 % + 3 × Yr2 % + 5 × Yr3%) ÷ 9
1:3 Overall mark = Yr2 % × 25% + Yr3 × 75%
1:2 Overall mark = Yr 2 × 0.33 + Yr3 × 0.67

If you are not given an equation then you need to multiply each percentage mark by its percentage weight and add the results together. For example:

A student scores 16 out of 20 in Test 1 and 32 out of 50 in Test 2. If the tests are weighted 25% for Test 1 and 75% for Test 2, what is the overall percentage?

Step i) 16/20 = 80%; 32/50 = 64%
Step ii) 80 × 25% = 20; 64 × 75% = 48
Step iii) 20 + 48 = 68%

3

Statistics

Maths audit 3

For the statistical questions you need to know the following:

- *Pie charts:* how to read data from a pie chart (multiply the total by the fraction shown).
- *Bar charts:* how to read data off a bar chart (read across to the vertical axis from the top of each bar).
- *Line graphs:* how to read data points on a line graph (read values off the horizontal and vertical axes).
- *Histograms:* how to read histograms created from tally charts and frequency tables.
- *Cumulative frequency graphs:* how to find the median, the upper quartile, the lower quartile; how many were below a given mark and how many were above a given grade.
- *Box and whisker plots:* how to use a box and whisker plot to identify six key pieces of information.
- *Tables:* how to locate information in tables and how to read two-way tables.

Most of the QTS numeracy questions in the 'on-screen' section involve charts, graphs or tables; they provide a simple and efficient way of displaying school data. You can expect to see a few easy questions, or 'one-liners' where the answer can be read directly from a chart or table. However, the majority of the answers require a careful interpretation of the question to locate the data, followed by the application of mathematical operations.

You are not expected to solve every problem in your head, in which case you will find it helpful to jot down a few numbers as you go along. If you need to use a calculator it is useful to have a rough idea of the size of the answer first. This book will not teach you how or when to use a calculator; you are expected to be able to key in the appropriate figures. Thus to work out 20% of 160,000 (see Figure 3.3) you would enter: 20 ÷ 100 × 160000 =. Alternatively you could short-cut this to 0.2 × 160000 or go one step further and work it out mentally as 2 × 16000.

Pie charts

These charts are not the most accurate way of displaying data but they do show at a glance the relative sizes of component parts. A full circle (360°) represents 100 percent of the data, so 180° = one-half (50%), 120° = one-third (33.3%) and 90° = one-quarter (25%), etc. Reading information from pie charts is easy but marks are lost when the candidate fails to look at the text in a key or sub-heading.

Now attempt the single-step questions associated with the two pie charts in Figures 3.1 and 3.2, for which a calculator is not required. You will need to use a calculator to answer some of the questions based on the single pie chart in Figure 3.3.

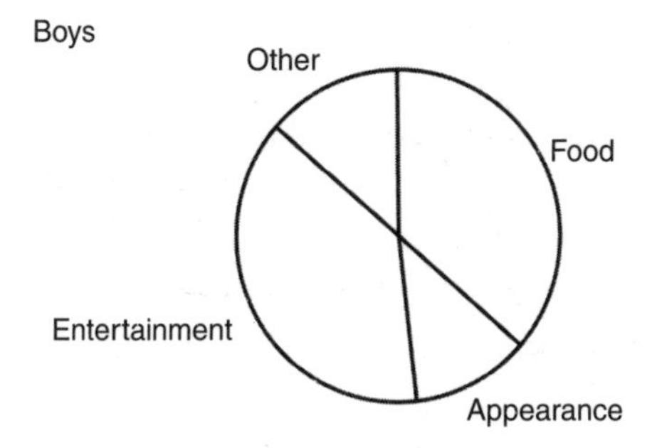

Figure 3.1 Distribution of boys' expenditure aged 7 to 15

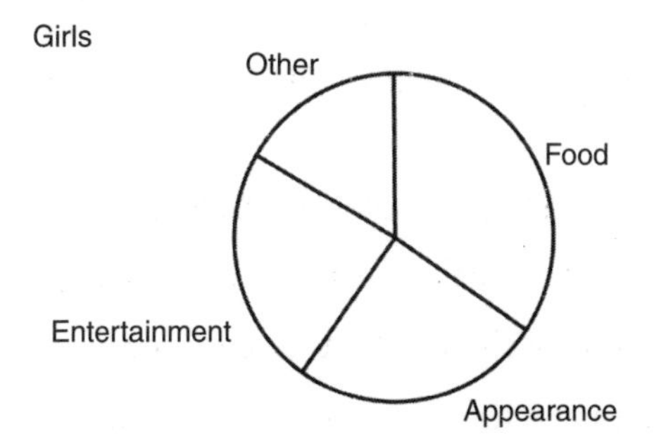

Figure 3.2 Distribution of girls' expenditure aged 7 to 15

Figures 3.1 and 3.2 example questions

1. What is the most popular area of girls' spending?
2. What is the least popular area of boys' spending?
3. In which area do boys and girls spend a similar proportion of their money?
4. What percentage of girls' spending is taken up by appearance (quarter circle)?
5. Girls spend twice as much as boys on appearance. What fraction of boys' expenditure is taken up by appearance?

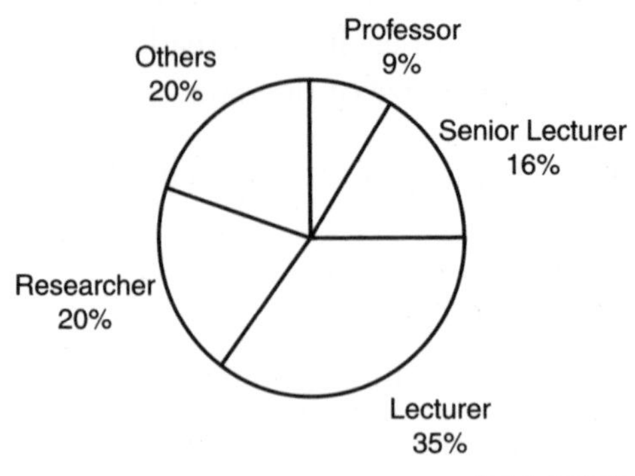

Figure 3.3 Grade of staff in higher education institutions

Figure 3.3 example questions (calculators are allowed)

1. What percentage of the staff are researchers?
2. What fraction of the staff are researchers?
3. What fraction of the staff are lecturer grade?
4. What fraction of the staff are senior lecturer grade?
5. What is the combined total of lecturers and senior lecturers as a decimal fraction of the whole?
6. How many staff are researchers?
7. How many more senior lecturers and researchers combined are there than lecturers?
8. How many staff are professors?
9. If there are five times as many male professors as female professors, how many female professors are there?

Bar charts

Bar graphs (bar charts) are useful for comparing different categories of data, for example GCSE subjects, or school results in different years. The bars can be drawn vertically or horizontally. The height (or length) of each bar is read off the scale on the axis and corresponds to the size of the data.

The bar graph in Figure 3.4 shows a school's seven most popular GCSE subjects.

Figure 3.4 example questions

1. Which subject is the most popular?
2. Which subject is the fifth most popular?
3. Which subject is three times more popular than History?
4. Which subject is two-thirds as popular as Science double?
5. What proportion of the total is taken up by English Literature? Give your answer as a fraction in its lowest terms and also as a decimal.

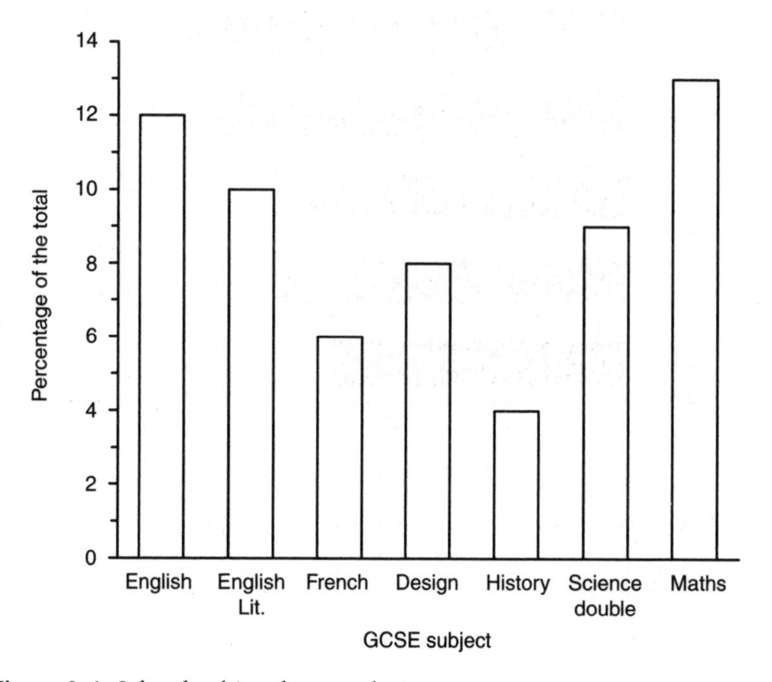

Figure 3.4 School subject by popularity

6. What proportion of the total is taken up by English and Maths together? Give your answer as a fraction in its lowest terms.
7. What is the ratio of pupils taking English Literature to pupils taking English? Give your answer in its lowest terms.
8. If 180 pupils take English, how many take English Literature?
9. What percentage of the total is taken up by all seven subjects?
10. What decimal fraction of the total is taken up by subjects other than those shown in the chart?

The bar chart in Figure 3.5 shows the percentage of pupils achieving grades A* to C in five popular subjects.

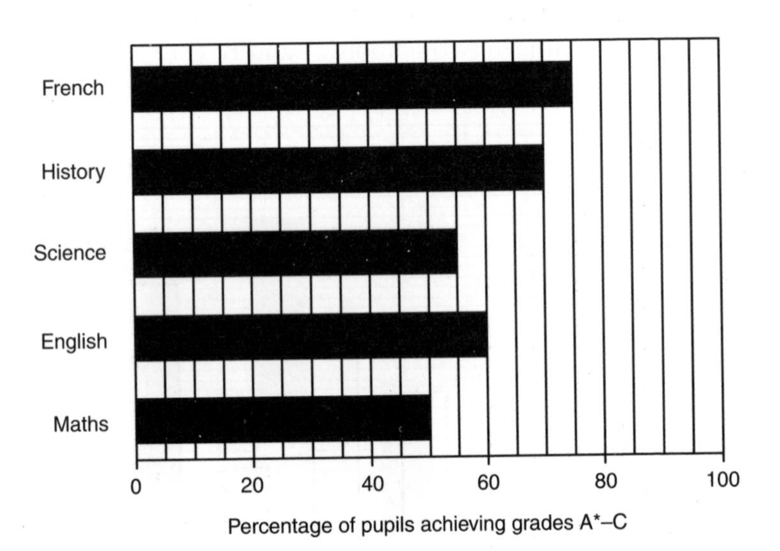

Figure 3.5 Bar chart of grades achieved in five subjects

Figure 3.5 example questions

1. If 180 pupils took GCSE Maths, how many achieved grades A* to C?
2. One-third as many pupils took History as took Maths. How many pupils achieved grades A* to C in History?
3. If English and Maths were equally popular, how many more pupils gained grades A* to C in English than in Maths?
4. If 54 pupils achieved grades A* to C in French, how many pupils took French?

In a stacked (compound) bar chart each bar is split into two or more segments that represent different data sets. The data are easier to compare than would be the case if the segments were shown as individual bars placed side by side. The stacked bar chart in Figure 3.6 compares pupils at Key Stage 2 achieving levels 2 to 5 in maths in two schools, A and B.

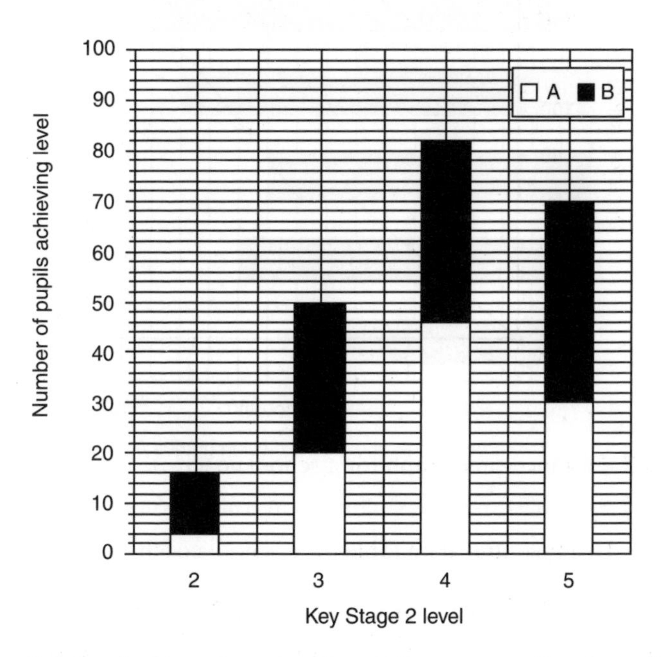

Figure 3.6 Stacked bar chart showing performance at Key Stage 2

Figure 3.6 example questions

1. At which level did school A outperform school B?
2. The graph shows that the number of pupils achieving level 2 at school B was three times that of school A (3:1 ratio). What was the B:A ratio for pupils achieving level 3?

Line graphs

With these graphs the data are plotted as a series of points joined by a line. Figure 3.7 shows a travel graph where the distance travelled in miles is plotted against the time in hours. The controlling quantity (time) is plotted on the x-axis and the quantity it controls (distance travelled) is plotted on the y-axis. The data table for the graph is shown in Table 3.1.

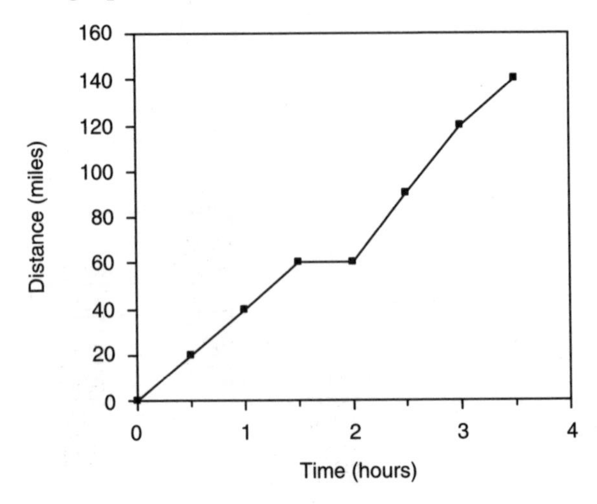

Figure 3.7 Distance-time graph for a school coach

Table 3.1 Distance-time data table for a school coach

Time (hours)	0	0.5	1.0	1.5	2.0	2.5	3.0	3.5
Dist. (miles)	0	20	40	60	60	90	120	140

Figure 3.7 example questions

1. What was the average speed for the journey?
2. For how many minutes was the coach stationary?
3. If the coach set out at 10.00 hrs, what was the average speed between midday and 1330 hrs, to the nearest mile per hour?
4. What are the x and y coordinates of the point at 13.00 hrs?

Multiple line graphs

Line graphs are useful for showing trends. Two or more lines can be shown together on the same axes to facilitate comparisons. The line graph in Figure 3.8 compares a local authority's A-level passes in Maths, Physics, Chemistry and Biology.

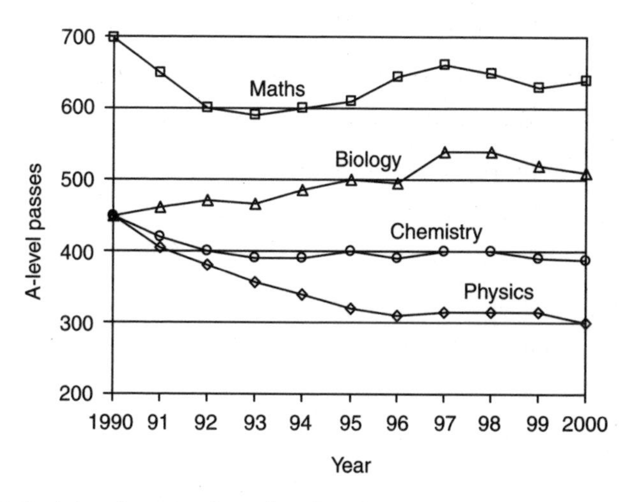

Figure 3.8 A-level passes for a local authority

Figure 3.8 example questions

1. Which subject showed the least variation in passes from 1990 to 2000 (least change)?
2. What was the range of the passes for Physics between 1990 and 2000 (maximum minus minimum)?

3. In 1995, how many more passes were there in Biology than in Chemistry?

4. Assuming the rate of decline in Maths passes from 1990 to 1992 had continued, how many Maths passes would have been predicted for the year 2000 (extend the line downwards or calculate the common difference)?

The graph in Figure 3.9 shows the percentage of pupils in a school achieving levels 5 to 8 and levels 3 to 8 in Maths at Key Stage 3.

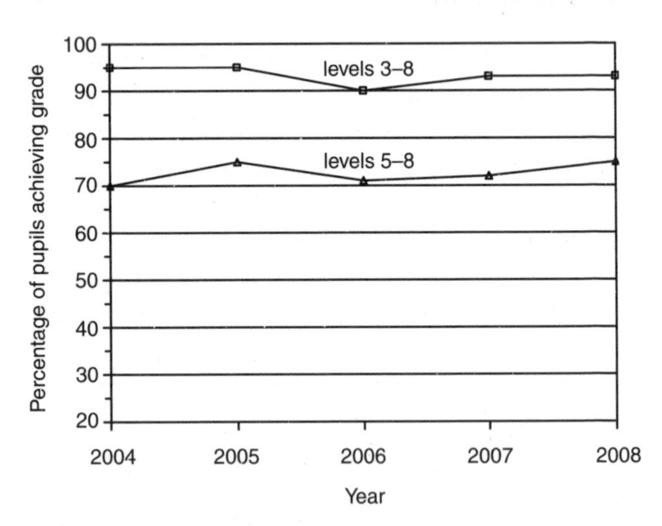

Figure 3.9 Pupil achievement at Key Stage 3 maths

Figure 3.9 example questions

1. What percentage of the pupils achieved levels 5 to 8 in 2004?

2. What percentage of the pupils achieved less than level 5 in 2004? (Hint: level 3–8 = 3, 4, 5, 6, 7, 8; level 5–8 = 5, 6, 7, 8.)

3. What fraction of the pupils achieved levels 5 to 8 in 2005? Give your answer in its lowest terms.

4. What fraction of the pupils achieved less than levels 5 in 2005? (Hint: level 3–8 = 3, 4, 5, 6, 7, 8; level 5–8 = 5, 6, 7, 8.)

Scatter graphs

These are similar to line graphs in that points are plotted and a line can be drawn. However, the line is not drawn from point to point but is a 'line of best fit' through all of the points. This 'regression line' can be judged by eye or it can be calculated. The line identifies any relationship (correlation) between the x and y values, as shown in the following examples:

a) Strong positive correlation; points lie close to a straight line (x and y increase in proportion to each other).

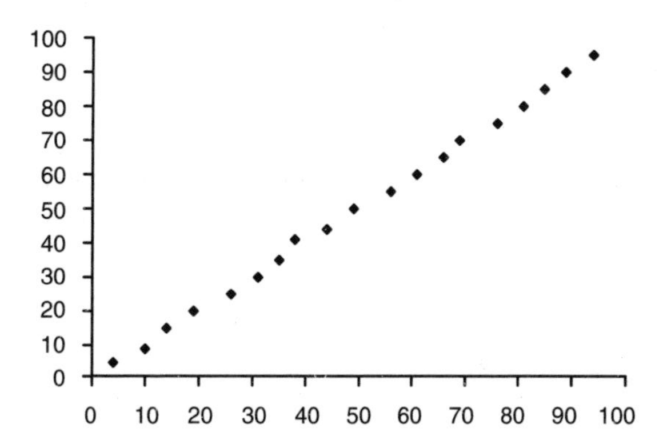

Figure 3.10 Strong positive correlation

b) Weak positive correlation; points are not close to a line.

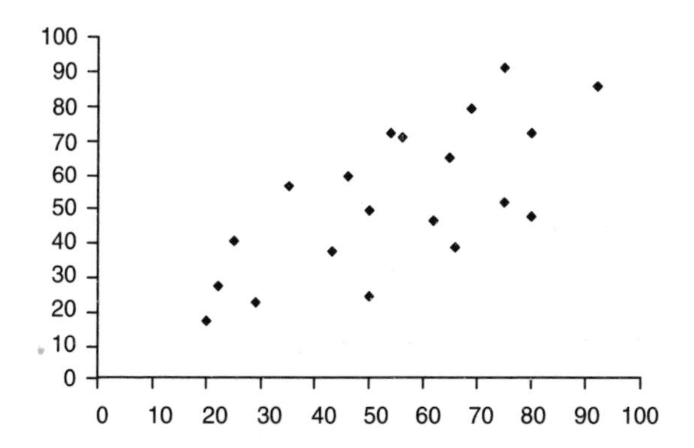

Figure 3.11 Weak positive correlation

c) No correlation; random (unable to predict x from y).

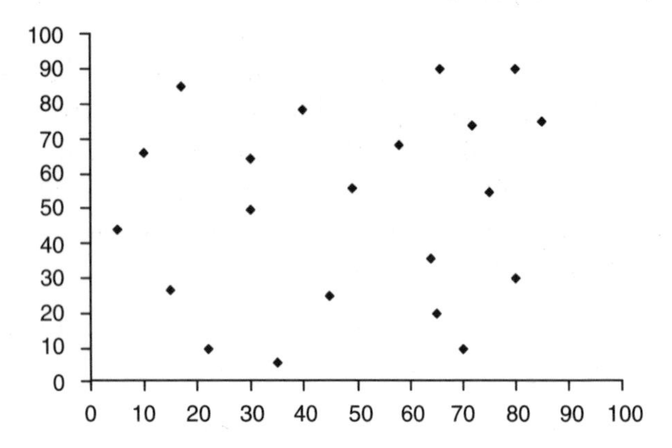

Figure 3.12 No correlation

Figure 3.13 is a scatter graph showing a strong negative correlation between Key Stage 2 performance and pupil absenteeism.

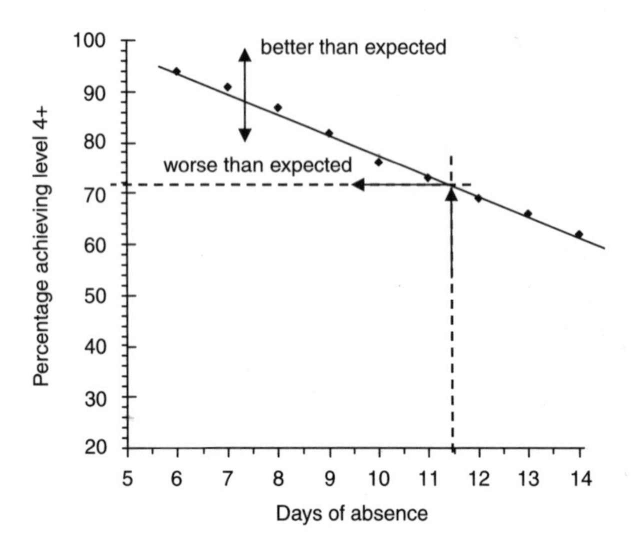

Figure 3.13 Strong negative correlation

Figure 3.13 example questions

1. What percentage of pupils would be expected to achieve level 4+ if they had 23 half-days of absence?
2. Pupils in a school have on average 10 days of absence each. If 70% achieve level 4 or above, is this better or worse than expected?
3. Pupils in a school have on average 8 days of absence each. If 90% achieve level 4 or above, is this better or worse than expected?

Figure 3.14 shows a scatter graph comparing results in an arithmetic test with results in a writing test.

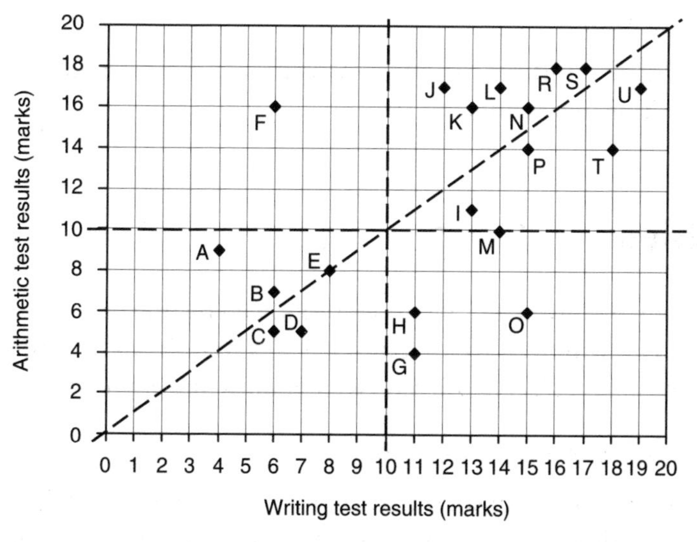

Figure 3.14 Scatter graph of arithmetic and writing test results

Figure 3.14 example questions

Use the three dashed lines to help you to determine:

1. Which pupil did equally well in both tests?
2. How many pupils did better in writing than in arithmetic?
3. How many pupils did better in arithmetic than in writing?
4. How many pupils gained 10 or more marks in arithmetic?
5. How many pupils gained 10 or more marks in writing?
6. How many pupils gained 10 or more marks in both writing and arithmetic?
7. How many pupils gained 10 or fewer marks in both writing and arithmetic?
8. Which pupil had the largest difference in arithmetic and writing test results?

Tables

Here you are given a table of data followed by one or more questions. You will need to look along a row and down a column to find the answer. Table 3.2 has two columns and eight rows.

Table 3.2 example questions

1. What is the total score for a pupil with an A grade in English, B grades in Sociology and Psychology, and C grades in Maths, History and Economics?
2. What is the average points score for the pupil in question 1? Give your answer to two decimal places.

Table 3.2 Points score versus GCSE grade (old system)

GCSE Grade	Points
A*	8
A	7
B	6
C	5
D	4
E	3
F	2
G	1

Example:
Pupil with 8 GCSEs
2 A grades = 2 × 7 = 14 points
3 B grades = 3 × 6 = 18 points
2 C grades = 2 × 5 = 10 points
1 D = 4 points
Total = 46 points
Average score = 46 ÷ 8 = 5.75

Table 3.3 looks very different but presents similar data in the form of eight columns and two rows.

Table 3.3 Points score versus GCSE grade (new system)

Grade	G	F	E	D	C	B	A	A*
Points	16	22	28	34	40	46	52	58

Table 3.3 example questions

A school can predict a pupil's GCSE grade in core subjects based on the level achieved at Key Stage 3 using the formula:

Point score = 6 × KS3 level + 3

1. How many points would be expected for a pupil with a level 7 in Maths at Key Stage 3?
2. What would be the most likely GCSE grade for the pupil in question 1?

3. A pupil gains a level 5 in English at Key Stage 3. What GCSE grade would be predicted?
4. A pupil is awarded GCSE grade B in Science. What level would you have expected at Key Stage 3?
5. A pupil gained level 7 in English and Science and level 6 in Maths. What were the pupil's average points?
6. What are the total points for a pupil achieving level 7 in eight subjects?
7. What are the average points for a pupil with two Bs, four Cs and two Ds?
8. A pupil has a total of 8 GCSEs, including five Cs and two Bs. If the points totalled 314, what was the other grade?

Two-way tables

These are useful for comparing pupil performance in two subjects (or in two different years). One subject occupies the columns and the other subject occupies the rows. The cells show the number of times the subjects are paired at each grade or level; all the combinations possible can be recorded. The table may also include the total number (summation) of the combinations across each row and column.

Table 3.4 compares the GCSE results of pupils who took both French (vertical column) and Spanish (horizontal row). Where a cell is empty the number of pupils obtaining that combination of grades is zero.

Table 3.4 Two way table forGCSE French and Spanish

	GCSE grade in French								
GCSE grade in Spanish	A*	A	B	C	D	E	F	G	Total
A*	1	2	1						4
A	1	2	1	1					5
B	1	2	3	2	1				9
C		1	2	4	2				9
D				2	1	1	1		5
E					1	1		1	3
F									0
G									0
Total	3	7	7	9	5	2	1	1	35

Table 3.4 example questions

1. How many pupils achieved a grade C in both French and Spanish?
2. How many pupils gained a grade C in Spanish?
3. How many pupils achieved a grade A in French?
4. How many pupils in total took both French and Spanish?
5. What was the modal grade for French?
6. How many pupils achieved grade C or above in Spanish?
7. What percentage of pupils achieved grade C or above in Spanish? (Give your answer to 1 decimal place.)
8. How many pupils achieved a lower grade in Spanish than in French (those left of a diagonal line from A*A* to GG)?

Tally charts, frequency tables and histograms

A tally chart is used to group and count data. The results are presented in a frequency table, and a frequency histogram (a bar chart of frequency distributions) is drawn. The histogram provides a mental picture of the spread of the marks with the most frequent marks normally centred on the middle. For example, 51 pupils achieved the following GCSE grades:

B C D E A B D C B A C C D C A* C E B A C B D C B C E D F D B C D B C D C F E C D B C D C D B C D C C B

The tally chart, frequency table and histogram are shown in Figure 3.15.

Tally chart

A*	I	1
A	III	3
B	卌 卌 I	11
C	卌 卌 卌 III	18
D	卌 卌 II	12
E	IIII	4
F	II	2

Frequency table

Grade	F	E	D	C	B	A	A*
Frequency	2	4	12	18	11	3	1

Histogram

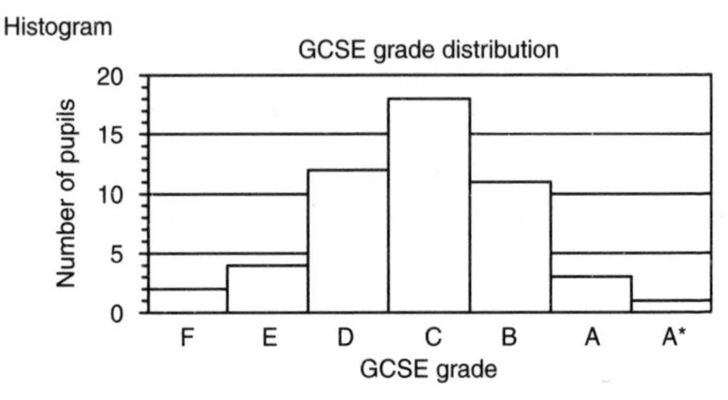

Figure 3.15 Tally chart, frequency table and histogram

The performance of a school can be assessed by allocating points to GCSE grades as described earlier and shown in Table 3.5. The frequency of the grades enables the total number of points to be calculated (points multiplied by frequency for every grade).

The mean value of all the points in the table is given by the total number of points divided by the total number of frequencies (total number of pupils):

Table 3.5 Allocating points to GCSE grades

Grade	F	E	D	C	B	A	A*
GCSE points	22	28	34	40	46	52	58
Frequency	2	4	12	18	11	3	1

$$\text{mean} = \frac{\text{‘total of’ [points multiplied by frequencies]}}{\text{‘total number of frequencies’}}$$

$$= \frac{(58\times1)+(52\times3)+(46\times11)+(40\times18)+(34\times12)+(28\times4)+ +(22\times2)}{1 + 3 + 11 + 18 + 12 + 4 + 2}$$

$$= \frac{58 + 156 + 506 + 720 + 408 + 112 + 44}{51}$$

$$= 2004 \div 51 = 39.29 \text{ points}$$

The mean points per pupil are 39.29 or just below grade C (40). The median points are those of the 26th pupil (middle of 51 is given by $(n + 1) \div 2 = 52 \div 2 = 26$th), found in the grade C group, ie median = 40 points. The modal points = 40 (most frequent points, 18 times).

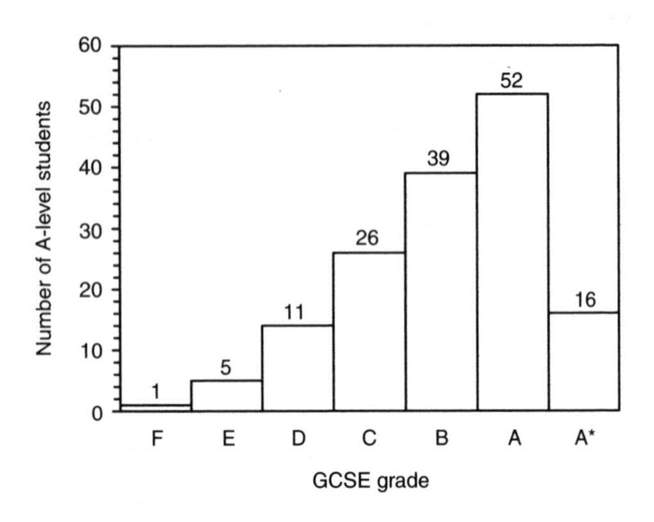

Figure 3.16 Histogram of GCSE grades for A-level students

Figure 3.16 example questions

1. How many students achieved GCSE grades A* to F
2. What percentage of the A*–F students achieved grade C or above? (Give your answer to 1 decimal place.)
3. What is the modal GCSE grade?
4. What is the median GCSE grade?
5. If 96% of the A-level students went on to higher education, how many students was this?

Histograms often group the marks into intervals, for example 10–19, 20–29, 30–39, etc to provide a clearer picture of the distribution of the marks; the bars should be touching because the data intervals are continuous.

The intervals can be described using the less than (<) and less than or equal to symbols (≤) to identify the boundaries of the marks:

symbol:	$n \leq 9$	$9 < n \leq 19$	$19 < n \leq 29$	$29 < n \leq 39$
interval:	0–9	10–19	20–29	30–39

Example: A sixth-form college converted the GCSE grades of 125 students to points. The points were averaged for each student to obtain a mean GCSE score (X); as shown in Table 3.6 and Figure 3.17.

Table 3.6 Example of intervals

Mean GCSE score (X)	Frequency
$4.5 < X \leq 5.0$	5
$5.0 < X \leq 5.5$	13
$5.5 < X \leq 6.0$	27
$6.0 < X \leq 6.5$	43
$6.5 < X \leq 7.0$	25
$7.0 < X \leq 7.5$	8
$7.5 < X \leq 8.0$	4

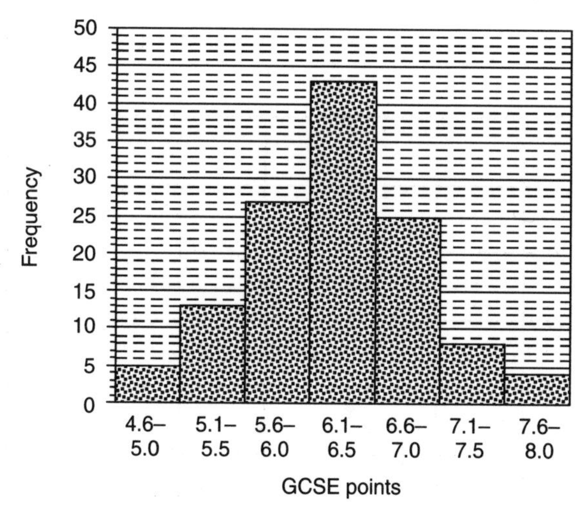

Figure 3.17 Histogram of GCSE points scores

Figure 3.17 example questions

1. What percentage of the students scored more than 6 points?
2. What is the ratio of students scoring more than 6 points to students scoring 6 points or less?
3. What percentage of the students scored in the range shown by $5.5 < X \leq 7.0$?

Cumulative frequency graphs

These are S-shaped graphs that show how many pupils achieved a particular grade and below. The running total of frequencies (not the actual frequency)is plotted against the grade. The final running total always equals the total number of pupils; as shown in Table 3.7.

Table 3.7 Cumulative frequency table

Grade	F	E	D	C	B	A	A*
Frequency	2	3	12	18	11	4	1
Cumulative frequency	2	5	17	35	46	50	51
	2	2+3	5+12	17+18	35+11	46+4	50+1

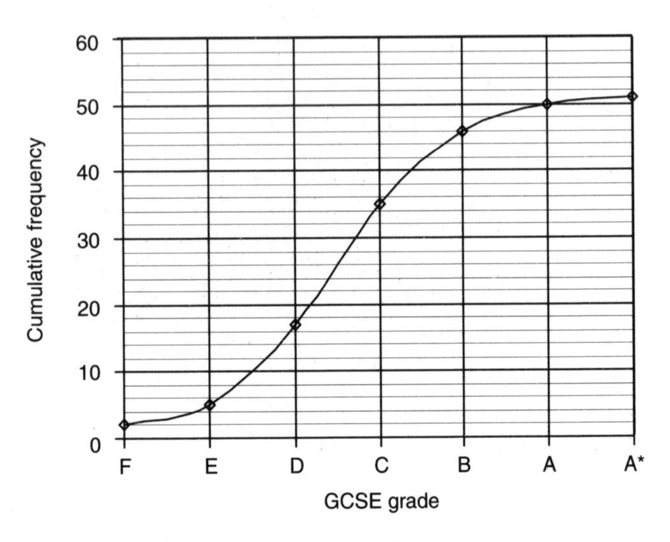

Figure 3.18 Cumulative frequency graph of GCSE grades

Figure 3.18 example questions

How many pupils achieved:

1. Grade C and below (ie up to grade C)?
2. Grade B and below (ie up to grade B)?
3. Grade A and below (ie up to grade A)?

There were 51 pupils in total. Refer to your answers in 1, 2 and 3 respectively to answer questions 4, 5 and 6.

How many pupils achieved:

4. Grade B and above?
5. Grade A and above?
6. Grade A*?
7. Grade C or above? (Hint: 51 minus grade D and below; or read from the table 18 + 11 + 4 + 1.)
8. Grade D or above?
9. What fraction of the pupils achieved grade C or above?
10. What percentage of the pupils achieved grade D or above? (Give your answer to 1 decimal place.)
11. What proportion of the pupils achieved grade B and above? (Give your answer to 1 decimal place.)

In the cumulative frequency graph in Figure 3.19 the GCSE grades have been converted to points, as shown in Table 3.8.

Table 3.8 Cumulative frequency table

Grade	F	E	D	C	B	A	A*
GCSE points	22	28	34	40	46	52	58
Frequency	1	2	9	26	42	60	20
Cumulative frequency	1	3	12	38	80	140	160

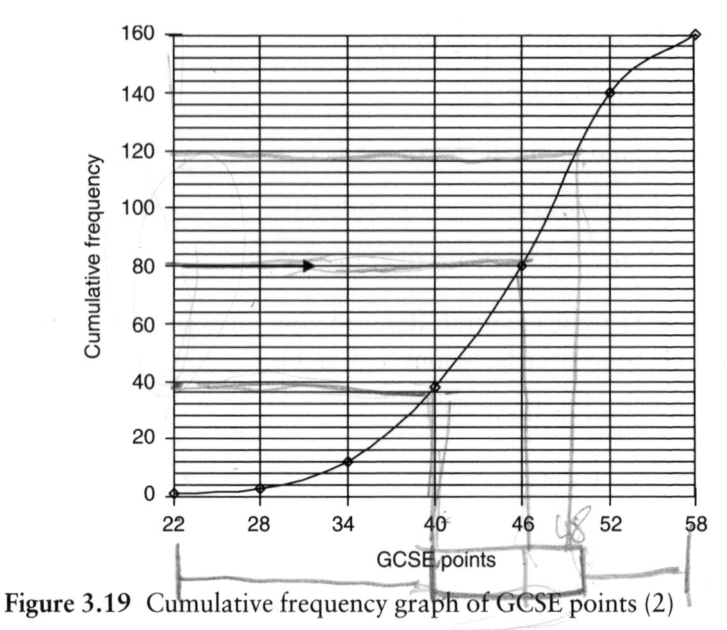

Figure 3.19 Cumulative frequency graph of GCSE points (2)

The median is the point's score of the middle student (80th) located half way up the cumulative frequency axis.

Figure 3.19 example questions

1. What is the highest GCSE point score?
2. What is the lowest GCSE points score?
3. What is the range of the GCSE points scores?
4. What is the median GCSE points score?
5. How many students achieved 52 points and below?
6. How many students achieved more than 52 points?
7. How many students achieved more than 34 points? (Read the y-axis scale carefully.)

One-hundred students took a QTS numeracy test. The cumulative frequency graph in Figure 3.20 shows the percentage of pupils achieving a given mark or less.

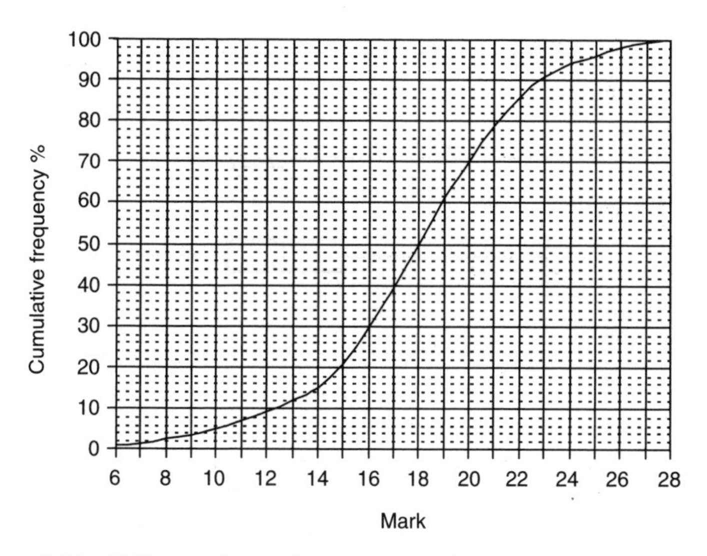

Figure 3.20 QTS cumulative frequency graph

Figure 3.20 example questions

1. The median mark can be read from the 50th percentile* (50% cumulative frequency). What mark does this correspond to?
2. Which mark did 70% of the students fall below?
3. Which mark did 12% of the students fall below?
4. How many students achieved 16 marks or lower?
5. The pass mark is 17 out of 28. How many students passed?

* Percentiles: dividing the data (marks) into 100 equal parts.

Box and whisker plots

These plots provide a method of visualizing several key pieces of statistical information including the maximum and minimum values, the median and the spread (distribution) of the values.

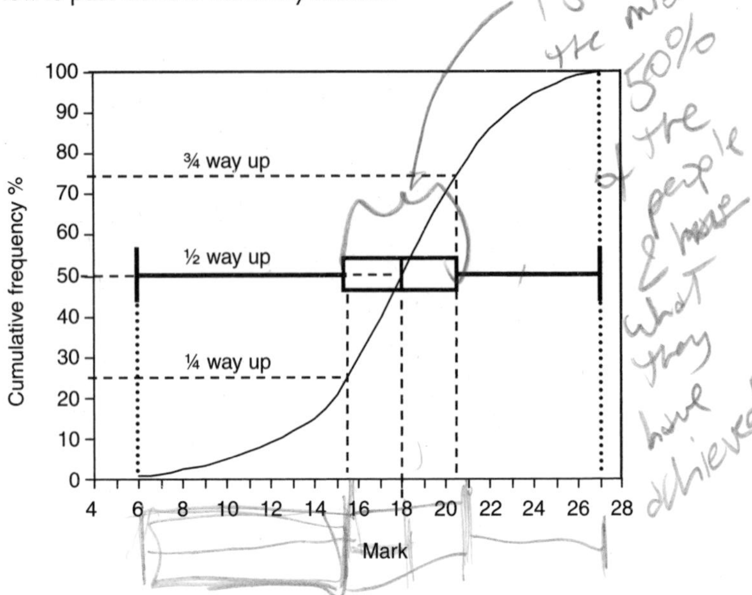

Figure 3.21 A box and whisker plot

Figure 3.21 shows a box and whisker plot drawn on the cumulative frequency chart shown in Figure 3.20.

The box and whisker plot summarizes seven key values based on splitting the data into four quarters, as shown in Figure 3.22.

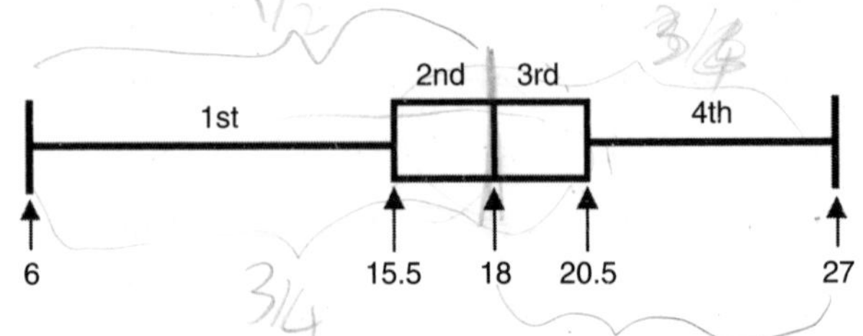

Figure 3.22 Splitting the data into four quarters

6: the lowest mark (end of whisker);
15.5: the lower quartile mark at the 25th percentile;
18: the median mark at the 50th percentile;
20.5: the upper quartile mark at the 75th percentile;
27: highest mark (end of whisker);
20.5–15.5: the inter-quartile range;
27–6: the range (end of one whisker to the end of the other).

Box and whisker plots can also be drawn vertically, as shown in Figure 3.23. The plots compare pupil performance in three subjects.

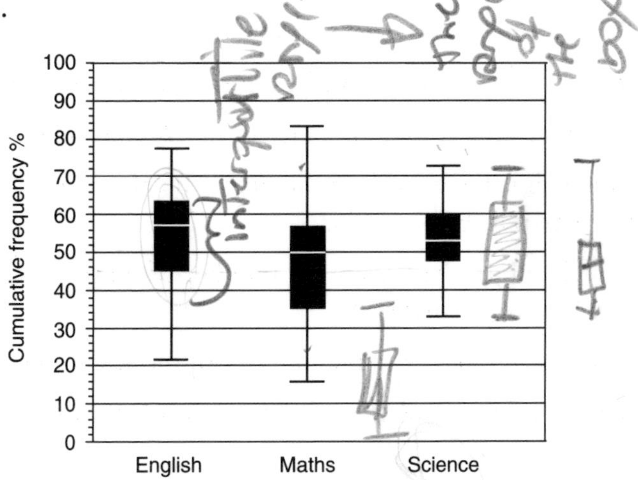

Figure 3.23 Vertical box and whisker plot for key subject exam results

The following points should be considered when answering the questions:

- The lower quartile is the mark below which one-quarter of the marks lie (it is the bottom 25% of the range) and three-quarters of the marks lie above it.
- The upper quartile is the mark above which one-quarter of the marks lie (it is the top 25% of the range) and three-quarters of the marks lie below it.
- The spread of the first and last quarters is shown by the length of the two whiskers drawn to the end points (the lowest mark and the highest mark).
- The spread of the two middle quarters is shown by the two boxes (each plot has two boxes and two whiskers) and represents the inter-quartile range.
- Half of the marks (50%) fall into the inter-quartile range.

Figure 3.23 example questions

1. Which subject had the lowest mark?
2. Which subject had the highest median mark?
3. Which subject had the smallest inter-quartile range?
4. In which subject was the range of marks the highest?
5. In which subject did half the marks lie above 54% and half the marks lie below 54%?
6. Which subject had a similar number of marks in the upper and lower quartiles?
7. Above what mark did one-quarter of the science marks lie?
8. Which subject had the widest range of marks for the top 25%?
9. If 80 pupils took the English test, how many were in the inter-quartile range?
10. Which subject had the highest proportion of pupils achieving 60% or more of the marks?

Introduction to the 'on-screen' type mock tests

In the second section of the test the questions appear on the screen. The following points are worth noting for the actual QTS test:

- Remember to use the on-screen calculator.
- Scroll forwards using the 'next' button and backwards using the 'previous' button to find the easier questions; plan to skip the more difficult questions, leaving them until the end of the test.
- Do not accidentally click on the 'end exam' button.
- The 'exhibit' button displays additional information.
- The clock shows the time remaining.
- There is no need to include units with your answers.
- The mouse is used for 'drag and drop' and 'point and click' answers.
- There is more time than you might think, so do not rush.

There now follow two mock 'on-screen' tests of 16 questions each. You have 35 minutes to complete each test, or just over two minutes per question. If you find any question difficult, skip it and return to it later. Make sure that you have a calculator to hand as well as a pen and paper.

Some questions will ask you to 'indicate all the true statements', in which case you tick the correct answer(s), or mark the statements True (T) and False (F), as per the answers at the end of the book. In the actual test you have to click inside a box to bring up a tick mark alongside the correct answer(s).

Mock test 1 (16 'on-screen' questions in 35 minutes)

Question 1

Temperatures in Celsius (C) can be converted to temperatures in Fahrenheit (F) using the following formula:

$F = [(C+40) \times 1.8] - 40$

What is 21°C converted to Fahrenheit? Answer [ ]

Question 2

A teacher summarized the marks in a maths test using the box and whisker plot below.

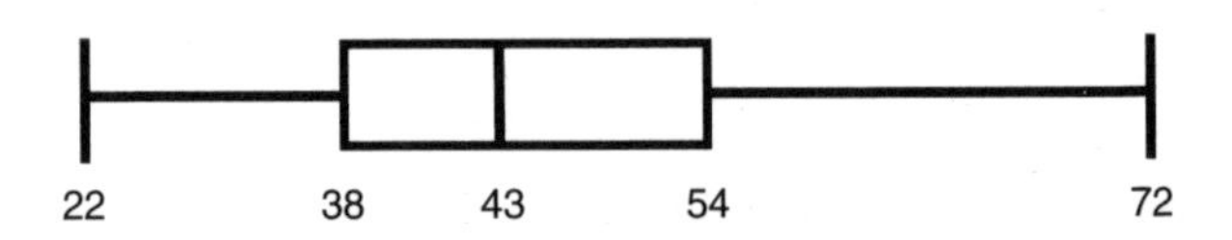

Indicate all the true statements:

1. At least one pupil achieved 72 marks. Answer [ ]

2. The inter-quartile range was 16. Answer [ ]

3. One-quarter of the pupils scored more than 38 marks. Answer [ ]

Question 3

The following table compares a school's A-level entries in Chemistry, Physics and Biology according to sex.

	Chemistry	Physics	Biology
Boys	36	45	30
Girls	32	10	50

Indicate all the true statements:

1. The ratio of boys to girls in Chemistry was 8:9. Answer

2. The ratio of girls to boys in Physics was 2:9. Answer

3. The ratio of boys to girls in Biology was 5:3. Answer

Question 4

The graph shows the cumulative frequency of a school's SPaG test results.

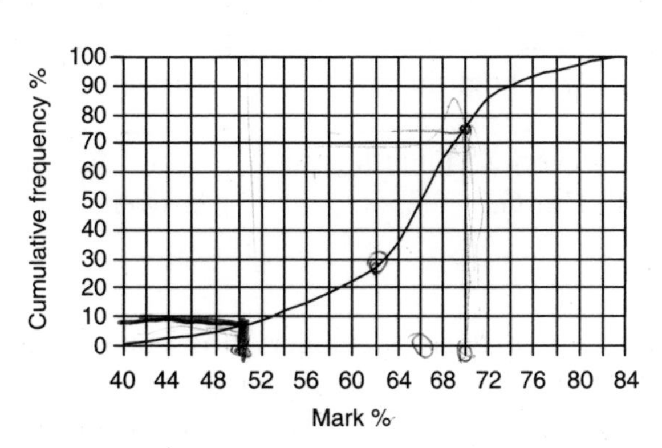

Indicate all the true statements:

1. The median mark was 50%. Answer

2. The upper quartile is at about 70% of the marks. Answer

3. At least 90% of the pupils achieved a mark above 50%. Answer

Question 5

The table shows a school's GCSE grade distribution in core subjects.

	Maths	English	Science
A*–C	89%	92%	95%
A*–G	96%	100%	98%

Indicate all the true statements:

1. 11% of maths pupils failed to achieve a grade C or above. Answer [ ]

2. The number of pupils achieving grade A*–C in Science was higher than the number achieving grades A*–C in English. Answer [ ]

3. Two out of every 25 English grades were D, E, F or G. Answer [ ]

Question 6

On a school trip to Paris a teacher runs out of Euros. She exchanges £200 for Euros at an exchange rate of 13 Euros for every £10. The teacher spends 195 Euros and at the end of the trip exchanges the remaining Euros back into pounds at the same exchange rate. How many pounds does she have?

Answer [ ]

Question 7

The pie charts show the distribution of A-level grades in two different schools, A and B.

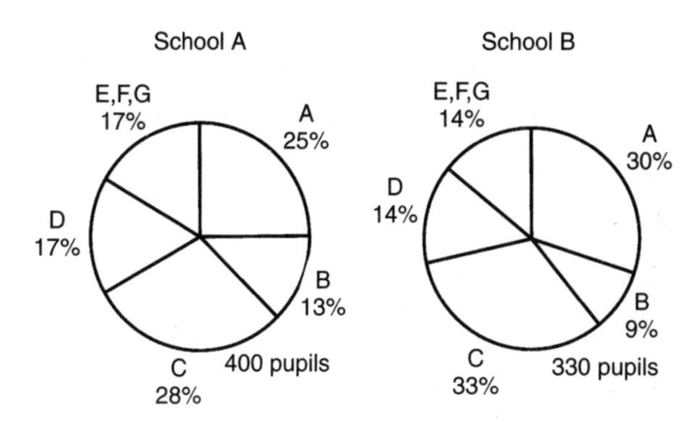

Indicate all the true statements:

1. School B achieved more A grades than School A. Answer

2. The number of pupils achieving grade C or above in School A was 264. Answer

3. The A–C pass rate in School B was 6% above that in School A. Answer

Question 8

The table shows the percentage of pupils achieving Level 4 and above at Key Stage 2 English, Maths and Science between 2001 and 2005.

	Pupils achieving level 4+ at Key Stage 2 (%)		
Year	English	Maths	Science
2001	75	71	87
2002	75	73	86
2003	75		87
2004	77	74	86
2005	79	75	86
Mean		73.2	86.4

Indicate all the true statements:

1. The mean for English for the five year period was 76.2%. Answer ☐

2. 72% of Maths pupils achieved level 4 or above in 2003. Answer ☐

3. For science for the five-year period the mode was 86% and the median was 86.5%. Answer ☐

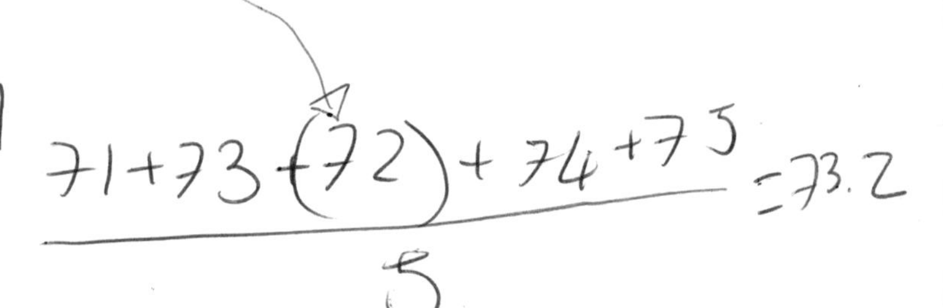

Question 9

The table shows test scores in reading, writing and arithmetic.

	Reading score (out of 40)	Writing score (out of 50)	Arithmetic score (out of 60)
Lowest	15	18	25
Median	29	36	47
Highest	36	43	54

Which test had the highest percentage mark and the smallest range?

Answer Reading

Question 10

Photocopying paper weighs 80 g/m^2. The dimensions of a single sheet are 21 cm x 30 cm. What is the weight of a five-ream box of paper, in kilograms? (1 ream = 500 sheets.)

Answer

Question 11

The bar chart shows Key Stage 2 Level 4 performance in English versus the proportion of pupils eligible for free school meals in an LEA's schools for 2000 and 2004.

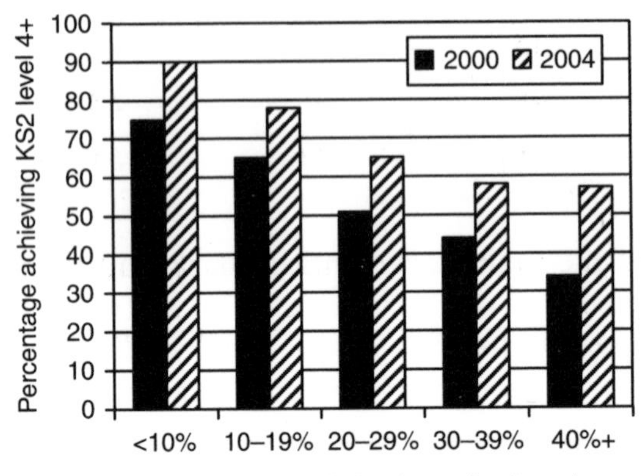

Indicate all the true statements:

1. The percentage of pupils achieving KS2 Level 4 in English in 2004 was above that for 2000.

   Answer

2. The schools with the highest proportion of pupils on free school meals showed the greatest improvements in KS2 performance from 2000 to 2004.

   Answer

3. In 2004, less than 10% of the pupils achieved KS2 Level 4+ in schools where 90% were entitled to free school meals.

   Answer

Question 12

The table shows pupil performance at the end of Key Stage 3 English, Maths and Science.

Name	English KS3 Level	Maths KS3 Level	Science KS3 Level
Aziz	6	5	5
Bethan	5	4	5
Carl	5	5	6
Eleri	4	6	4
Harry	5	5	6
Josh	5	4	5
Phoebe	7	7	7
Ruby	5	5	6
Yasmin	4	4	5
Zak	6	6	5
% at level 5 or above		70	90
% at level 6 or above	50	60	30

1. What percentage of the pupils achieved Level 5 or above in English?

   Answer

2. What proportion of the pupils who achieved Level 5 or above in Science also achieved Level 5 or above in Maths? Give your answer as fraction in its lowest terms.

   Answer

3. What proportion of the pupils achieved Level 5 or above in all three subjects? Give you answer as a percentage.

   Answer

Question 13

Pupils are taken on a field trip to Ireland via the Holyhead–Dublin Ferry. The Ferry timetable is shown below.

	Holyhead to Dublin		Dublin to Holyhead	
Vessel	Departs	Arrives	Departs	Arrives
Cruise	0240	0555	0805	1130
Swift	1200	1355	0845	1045
Cruise	1410	1525	1430	1630
Swift	1715	1915	2055	0020
	Latest check-in time is 30 minutes before departure			

What is the latest check-in time if the pupils are to arrive back in Holyhead before midday?

Answer

Question 14

The graph shows the percentage of pupils at Key Stage 1 Maths Level 3 from 2002 to 2007 for a school and its local authority.

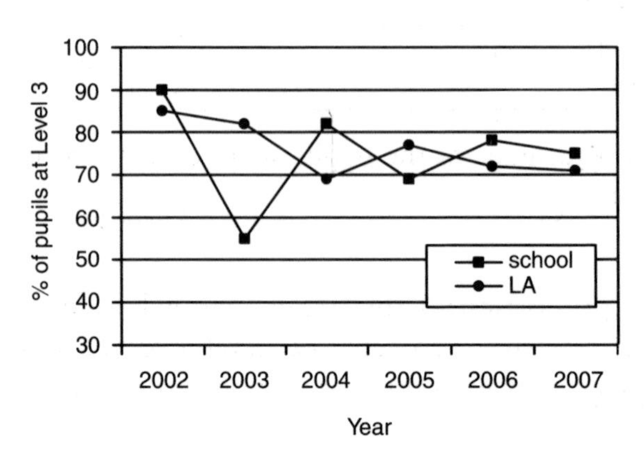

In which year did the school's performance exceed that of the local authority by more than 10%?

Answer

Question 15

A pupil sat four tests, namely Test 1A, Test 1B, Test 2A and Test 2B. The test results and the weightings are shown below.

	Test %		Weighting		
	A	B	A	B	Combined %
Test 1	70%	36%	50%	50%	
Test 2	60%	40%	70%	30%	

Calculate the combined percentage (A plus B) for Test 1 and Test 2. Select your answers from the following four choices: 55%, 54%, 53%, 52%.

Answer 1.

Answer 2.

Question 16

The bar graph shows the percentage of pupils in a school who achieved GCSE grade C or above in five subjects, by sex.

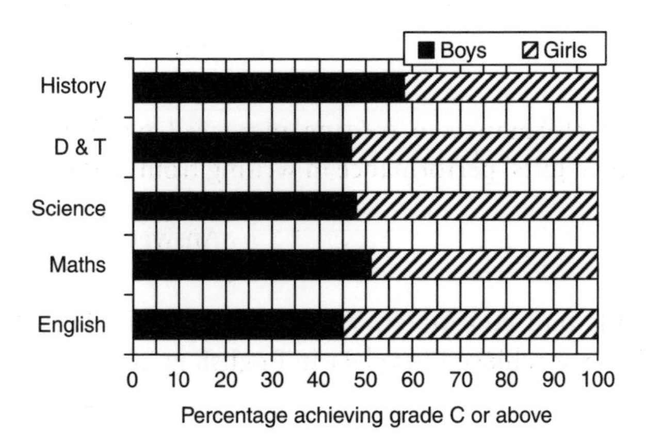

What proportion of the pupils who achieved grade C or above in English are boys? Give your answer as a fraction.

Answer

Mock test 2 (16 'on-screen' questions in 35 minutes)

Question 1

The table shows the percentages of a school's pupils achieving Level 4 or above in teacher assessments, by sex, 2004–2006.

	Percentage of pupils at Level 4+					
	Boys			Girls		
	2004	2005	2006	2004	2005	2006
English	72	74	76	84	84	84
Reading	79	82	80	87	87	87
Writing	55	56	60	71	72	75
Maths	73	75	77	74	75	75

Indicate all the true statements:

1. The percentage of pupils achieving Level 4+ in each test from 2004 to 2006 was greater for girls than for boys.

Answer

2. Boys' performance in writing increased proportionately more than girls' performance in writing from 2004 to 2006.

Answer

3. If trends had continued, 78% of boys and 84% of girls would have achieved Level 4+ in English in 2007.

Answer

Question 2

The table shows the number of pupils using different modes of transport to a school.

Car	Bus	Cycling	Walking	Other
	31	20	67	11

One pupil in every four travels to school by car. How many pupils travel to school by car?

Answer

Question 3

The pie chart shows the distribution of marks available in an English test.

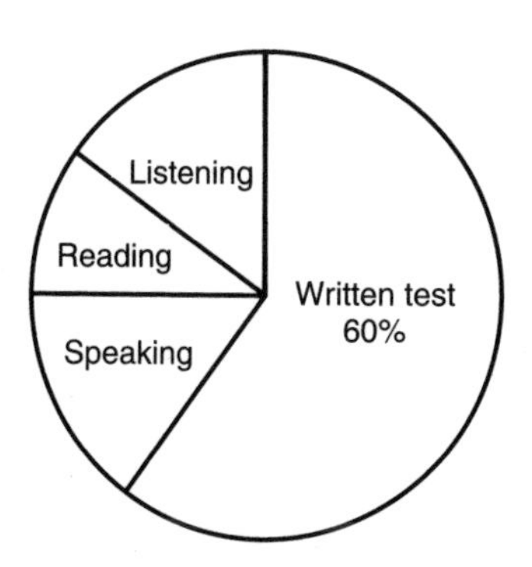

A pupil scored 75% in the written test and averaged 65% in the remaining tests. What was his overall percentage mark?

Answer

Question 4

A primary school calculates its Pupil/Teacher Ratio (PTR) by dividing the number of pupils by the number of teachers. The number of teachers includes the Principal and any part-time staff. For part-time staff the full-time teaching equivalent is given by: part-time hours ÷ 25.

Calculate the PTR of a school with 170 pupils where the Principal has seven full-time teachers and one part-time teacher working 15 hours. Give your answer to one decimal place.

Answer

Question 5

A school compared Key Stage 2 points score with Key Stage 3 marks.

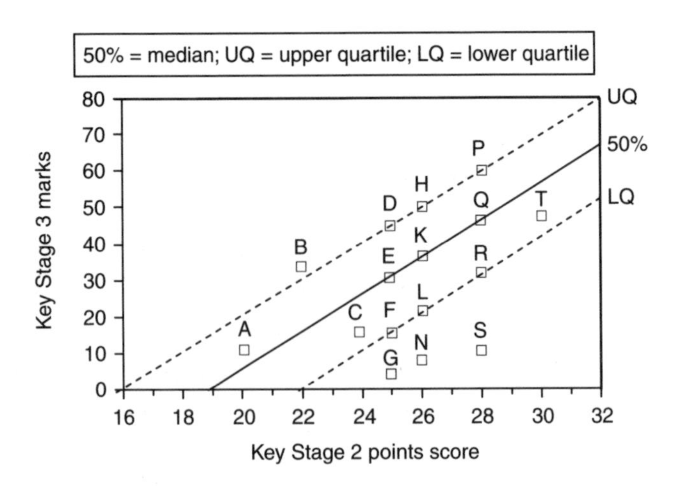

Choose the letter of the pupil that fits the description given.

1. This pupil scored 25 points at Key Stage 2 and the middle mark at Key Stage 3.

Answer

2. One-quarter of the pupils with 28 points at Key Stage 2 have Key Stage 3 marks above this pupil.

Answer

3. Three-quarters of the pupils with 26 points at Key Stage 2 have Key Stage 3 marks above this pupil.

Answer

Question 6

A pupil takes £100 on a school trip to Poland and exchanges £80 for Polish zlotys (zl) at an exchange rate £1.00 = 4.25 zl. He spends 250 zl in Poland and then exchanges the balance of his zlotys back into pounds at a rate of 4.50 zl = £1.00. How much money does he have on returning home?

Answer

Question 7

In a school's charity project, shoeboxes are covered in wrapping paper and filled with gifts. One shoebox is shown below.

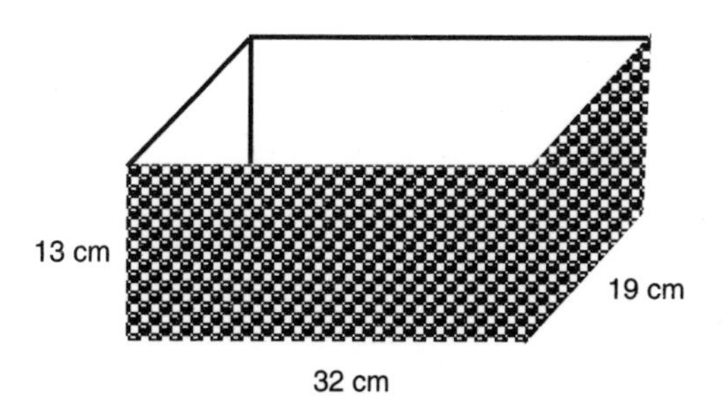

What is the minimum length of wrapping paper needed to cover all four sides of the box with a 2 cm overlap at the join? Give your answer in metres.

Answer

Question 8

A teacher set up a spreadsheet to calculate the cost of school trips, then entered the data for a farm trip.

	A	B	C	D
1	Items	Cost/item	Number	£ Total
2	Bus hire	176.00	1	176.00
3	Fee pupil	3.50	24	84.00
4	Fee adult	5.00	4	20.00
5				
6				
7		Total cost		280.00
8		Cost/person		10.00

Calculate the cost per person of the same farm trip with bus hire costing 6% more and fees costing 10% more.

Answer [ ]

Question 9

A pupil displayed his coursework data in a bar chart and a pie chart.

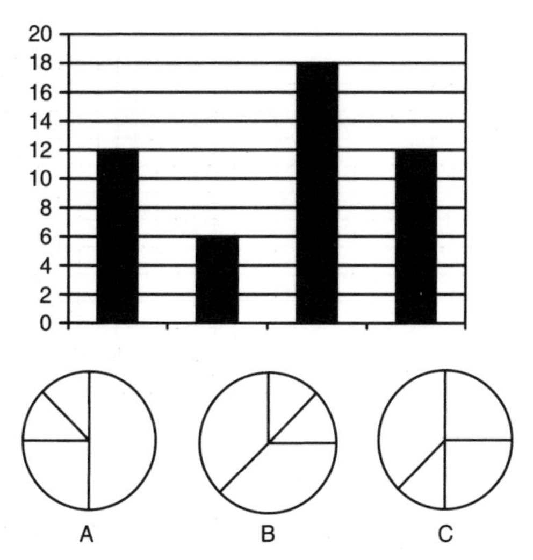

Which pie chart shows the same data as the bar chart?

Answer

Question 10

The table shows the distribution of pupils in a school according to year group.

Year	7	8	9	10	11	12	13	Total
Number	185	184	181	180			120	

How many pupils are on roll at the school if the mean number of pupils in years 7 to 11 is 181 and the ratio of pupils in year 11 to year 12 is 7:5?

Answer

Question 11

The graph shows the cumulative frequency of the hours spent on homework per week by a school's year 10 pupils.

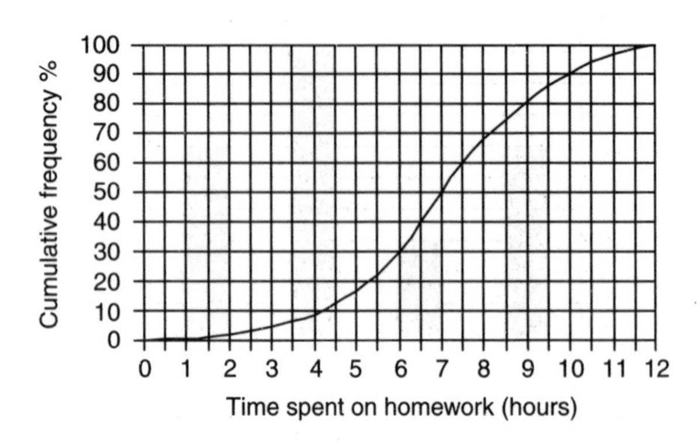

Indicate all the true statements:

1. Most of the pupils spent up to 7 hours on homework.

Answer

2. About 90% of pupils spent at least 4 hours on homework.

Answer

3. The lower quartile is less than 6 hours.

Answer

Question 12

Six schools had the following proportion of pupils on free meals.

School	Proportion
A	10 out of 190
B	14%
C	1/9
D	0.06
E	1/20
F	17 out of 250

Which school had the highest proportion of pupils on free meals and which school had the lowest proportion on free meals?

Answer [ ] [ ]

Question 13

The scatter graph shows achievement at A-level plotted against prior achievement at GCSE.

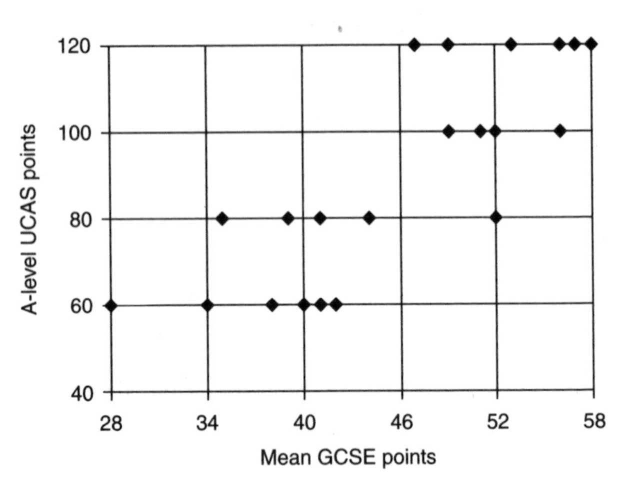

Indicate all the true statements:

1. Two students achieved 120 points at A-level and less than 52 mean GCSE points.

   Answer [ ]

2. Two-thirds of the students averaged less than 52 GCSE points.

   Answer [ ]

3. All the students with mean GCSE points of 46 or more achieved at least 100 points at A-level.

   Answer [ ]

Question 14

A school coach plans to leave Paris to arrive in Calais no later than 12.30 hours. The coach averages 50 miles per hour and the distance from Paris to Calais is 300 kilometres. Use the approximation of 5 miles = 8 kilometres to find the latest time the coach can leave Paris.

Answer

Question 15

The table shows the GCSE grades achieved by Science pupils in classes 11a, 11b and 11c.

	Number of pupils gaining each grade		
Grade	Class 11a	Class 11b	Class 11c
A*	1	2	0
A	4	3	0
B	6	4	4
C	7	9	11
D	3	4	7
E	3	2	2
F	0	1	1
G	1	0	0
Total	25	25	25

Choose the letter (P, Q, R, S or T) in the next table that shows the correct A* to C results for the Science pupils shown above.

	Mean number of pupils gaining A* to C				
Mode	P	Q	R	S	T
A*	13	14	15	16	17
A	14	15	16	17	18
B	15	16	17	18	19
C	16	17	18	19	20
D	17	18	19	20	21
E	18	19	20	21	22
F	22	23	24	25	26
G	27	28	29	30	31

Answer

Question 16

The bar chart shows the number of pupils with and without special educational needs (SEN) in four schools, A, B, C and D.

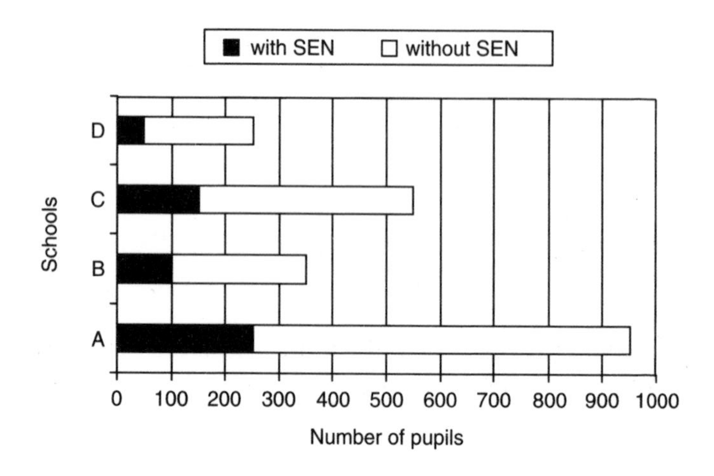

Which school had the highest proportion of pupils with special educational needs?

Answer

Answers

Mental arithmetic test 1

1. In a school of three-hundred and twenty-four pupils, one-sixth take free school meals. How many take free school meals?

   $324 \div 6 = 300 \div 6 + 24 \div 6 = 50 + 4 =$ **54**

2. A school library contains one-hundred and fifty-six books. If the number of non-fiction books is twice the number of fiction books, how many non-fiction books are there?

   $2n + n = 156$; $3n = 156$; $n = 52$; $2n =$ fiction = **104**

3. If one gallon is equivalent to four point five litres, how many gallons are there in one litre? Give your answer as a fraction.

   1 gal = 4.54 litre so 1 litre = $1 \div 4.5$ gal = $2 \div 9 =$ **2/9 gal**

4. A school can buy ten books at nine pounds and ninety-five pence each or borrow the books from a library service at a cost of forty pounds. How much money will be saved by borrowing the books?

   $9.95 \times 10 - 40 = 99.50 - 40 =$ **£59.50**

5. A school audio CD costs five pounds plus VAT. If VAT is charged at seventeen and one-half percent, how much does the CD cost to the nearest penny?

   17.5% = 17.5 p per pound (per 100p)
   $17.5 \times 5 = 18 \times 5 - 0.5 \times 5 = 90 - 2.5 = 87.5$ p = 88p
   + £5 = **£5.88**

6. Two hundred and forty pupils sat GCSE English. If forty-five percent of the pupils achieved grade D or below, how many achieved grade C or above?

   $100\% - 45\% = 55\%$; $55\% \times 240 = 50\% \times 240 + 5\% \times 240$
   $= 120 + 12 =$ **132**

7. A school bus arrives at the Tate Gallery at twelve hundred hours. The journey took two hours and twenty-five minutes excluding a fifteen minute break. At what time did it set out?

   Total time taken = 2 hr 25 min + 15 min = 2 hrs 40 min
   1200 hr – 2hr 40 min = 1200 hr – 3hr + 20 min = **0920**

8. In a school run a pupil completed five miles around a four hundred metre track. How many laps of the track were completed if one mile is taken to be one point six kilometres?

   5 miles = $5 \times 1.6 = 0.5 \times 16 = 8$ km
   8 km = 8×1000 m = 8000 m
   $8000 \div 400 = 80 \div 4 =$ **20 laps**

9. A ski trip to Switzerland cost seven hundred and fifty pounds and requires a twenty percent deposit. What is the deposit in Swiss francs if one pound is equivalent to two Swiss francs?

   £750 × 20% = 1/5 × £750 = £150 (or £750 × 0.2 = £75 × 2)
   £150 × 2 Swiss francs per pound = **300 francs**

10. What is thirty-seven and one-half percent as a fraction?

    37.5% = 37.5/100 = 75/200 = 15/40 = **3/8**

11. A school playground measures twelve metres by thirteen point five metres. What is its area in metres squared?

    12 × 13.5 = 12 × 10 + 12 × 3 + 12 × 0.5
    = 120 + 36 + 6 = 156 + 6 = **162 m^2**

12. An 11–18 comprehensive school has fifteen hundred and fifty pupils on roll, including three hundred and ten A-level students. What percentage of the pupils on roll are A-level students?

    310 ÷ 1550 × 100% = 310 ÷ 155 × 10 = 2 × 10 = **20%**

Mental arithmetic test 2

1. School dinners cost one pound and eighty-five pence each. A pupil pays in advance for a week's dinners. What is the correct change out of a ten pound note?

   £1.85 × 5 = £2 × 5 – 15p × 5 = £10 – 75p; change = **75p**

2. A school with nine hundred and fifty places has an occupancy rate of ninety-four percent. How many more pupils can it take?

   6%: 0.06 × 950 = 6 × 9.5 = 6 × 10 – 6 × 0.5 = 60 – 3 = **57**

3. A school has two hundred and ninety boys and three hundred and ten girls. How many girls would you expect there to be in a representative sample of one hundred and twenty pupils?

   290 + 310 = 600; 120 = 1/5 of 600
   1/5 × 310 = 1/5 × 300 + 1/5 × 10 = 60 + 2 = **62**

4. An exam finished at twelve twenty-five hours having lasted one and three-quarter hours. At what time did the exam start?

   1225 hrs – 1 hr 45 min = 1225 hrs – 2 hrs + 15 min = **1040**

5. In a sponsored run a pupil completed twenty laps around a four hundred metre track. How many miles did he complete if one kilometre equals five-eighths of a mile?

   20 × 400 = 8000 m = 8 km
   8 km × 5/8 miles/km = **5 miles**

6. In a secondary school with nine hundred pupils, four out of every five pupils own a mobile phone. How many pupils do not own a mobile phone?

   no phone = 1 out of 5 = 2 out of 10 = 20 out of 100
   20 × 9 = **180** (avoids fractions, decimals, percentages)

7. A sponsored walk by five hundred pupils raised six thousand, nine hundred and fifty pounds for charity. What was the average amount raised per pupil?

   6950 ÷ 500 = 6950 × 2 ÷ 1000
   6950 × 2 = 7000 × 2 – 50 × 2 = 14000 – 100 = 13900
   ÷ 1000 = **£13.90**

8. A school trip to the Tate Gallery took two hours and fifteen minutes by coach, travelling at an average speed of forty miles per hour. How far away was the gallery?

   2 hours and 15 minutes = 2.25 hours
   2.25 hours × 40 miles per hour = 22.5 × 4 = 88 + 2 = **90 miles**

9. A pupil gained thirty marks out of fifty in one Maths test and sixteen marks out of twenty-five in a second Maths test. What was the average percentage for the two tests assuming they were weighted equally?

   30 out of 50 = 30 × 2 out of 100 = 60% (or 30/50 × 100%)
   16 out of 25 = 16 × 4 out of 100 = 64% (or 16/25 × 100%)
   average = **62%**

10. What is sixty-two and one-half percent as a decimal fraction to one decimal place?

    62.5% = 62.5 ÷ 100 = 0.625 = **0.63** (to 1 dp)

11. A school skiing trip costs seven hundred and twenty pounds per pupil with a fifteen percent deposit. How much is the deposit in Euros if there are one point two-five Euros to the pound?

    $15\% \times £720 = 0.15 \times 720 = 15 \times 7.2 = 72 + 36 = £108$
    $£1 = €1.25$; $£108 = £108 \times 1.25€/£ = €108 + €108 \div 4$
    $= 108 + 27 =$ **€135**

12. Teachers at a school have four hours and twelve minutes contact time per day. What is the contact time per week?

    4 hr × 5 + 12 min × 5 = 20 hr + 60 min = **21 hrs**

Mental arithmetic test 3

1. A pupil aged eleven years and four months has a reading age eighteen months below his actual age. What is his reading age?

   subtract 18 months = subtract 2 years then add 6 months = **9 years 10 months**

2. A geography school trip costs seventy pounds and the deposit is fourteen pounds. What percentage of the cost is the deposit?

   14/70 × 100% = 14/7 × 10 = 2 × 10 = **20%**

3. Out of one hundred and forty-four pupils who sat GCSE English Literature, ninety achieved grades A to C. What fraction achieved grades A to C?

   90/144 = 45/72 = 15/24 = **5/8**

4. In a primary school, five percent of half-day sessions were missed through absence. If there were three-hundred and eighty half-day sessions, how many were missed through absence?

   10% × 380 = 38 half days so 5% = **19 half days**

5. How many school books at eight pounds and seventy-five pence each can be bought on a budget of one hundred pounds?

   100 ÷ 8.75 = 400 ÷ (32 + 3) = 400 ÷ 35 = 10 + 1 = **11**

6. The highest mark in a Maths test was forty-six correct answers out of fifty questions and the lowest mark was twenty-five correct answers out of fifty questions. What is the difference between the highest and lowest marks in percentage points?

   difference = 46 – 25 = 21 marks out of 50 = **42%**

7. A ski trip to Switzerland costs eight hundred pounds per pupil and requires a twenty-five percent deposit. What is the deposit in Swiss francs if one hundred pounds buys two hundred and five Swiss francs?

   £800 × 25% = 1/4 × £800 = £200
   £200 × 205 francs per £100 = 205 × 2 = **410**

8. What is four-fifths as a percentage?

   4 ÷ 5 × 100% = **80%**

9. A fence is to be erected around a school playing field. The field is rectangular in shape and measures one hundred and twenty metres by ninety metres. What length of fence will be needed?

   120 × 2 + 90 × 2 = 240 + 180 = **420 m**

10. What is two point five percent as a fraction in its lowest terms?

    2.5% = 2.5/100 = 5/200 = **1/40**

11. The teacher to pupil ratio on a school trip is not to be less than one to fifteen. If there are one hundred and seventy-two pupils going on the trip, how many teachers will be required?

    1:15 = 10:150 = 11:165 = 12:180 = **12**

12. A school day starts at eight-fifty am and finishes at three-thirty pm. Breaks total one hour and fifteen minutes. What is the maximum number of half-hour lessons possible per day?

    0850 hrs add 10 min add 6 hr add 30 min to reach 1530 hrs
    so lesson time = 6 hr 40 min – 1 hr 15 min breaks
    = 5 hr 25 min = **10 lessons max**

Mental arithmetic test 4

1. At the start of a school day the library contains twelve thousand books. By the end of the day one hundred and twenty-three books have been loaned out and fifty-seven books have been returned. How many books are there in the library at the end of the day?

   $12000 + 57 - 123 = 11900 + 157 - 123 = 11900 + 34 =$ **11934**
   (borrow 100 from 12000 to add to 57)

2. In a class of twenty-five pupils, forty percent are girls. How many boys are there in the class?

   $100\% - 40\% = 60\%; 0.6 \times 25 = 6 \times 2.5 = 12 + 3 =$ **15**

3. GCSE pupils take a Double Science or Single Science award. If Double Science is seven times more popular than the Single Science, what fraction of the pupils take Single Science?

   7 double + 1 single = 8 parts; single = **1/8** (double = 7/8)

4. The cost of a school ski trip was six hundred and sixty pounds per pupil last year. This year the cost will increase by three percent. What will be the cost per pupil this year? Give your answer to the nearest pound.

   $660 \times 3\% = 660 \times 3 \div 100 = 6.60 \times 3 =$ £18 + £1.80 = £19.80
   Cost = £660 + £19.80 = £679.80 = **£680**

5. What is zero point four five as a fraction?

   $0.45 = 45 \div 100 = 45/100 =$ **9/20**

6. In a year group, seven out of every ten pupils achieved Key Stage 2. What percentage of the pupils failed to achieve Key Stage 2?

   $7/10 \times 100\% = 70\%$ $100\% - 70\% =$ **30%**

7. How many pieces of card measuring thirty centimetres by twenty centimetres can be cut from a sheet measuring one point five metres by one point one metres?

   1.5 × 1.1 = 150 × 110 cm = 5 lengths × 5 widths = **25 pieces**

8. A pupil is one point six metres tall. If there are two point five centimetres to the inch, how tall is the pupil in inches?

   1.6 metres = 1.6 × 100 cm = 160 cm
   160 ÷ 2.5 = 1600 ÷ 25 = 6400 ÷ 100 = **64 inches**

9. School lessons start at a quarter past nine. There are ten lessons per day lasting thirty minutes each and breaks that total ninety minutes. What time does the school day finish?

   0915 + 5 hours lessons + 1.5 hr breaks = **1545 hrs**

10. A school minibus averages thirty miles per gallon. A teacher fills the tank with forty-five litres of fuel. How far can the minibus travel if one gallon is equivalent to four and one half litres?

    45 ÷ 4.5 = 10; 10 × 30 = **300 miles**

11. A test has a pass mark of seventy percent. If there are thirty-five questions, what is the minimum number of correct answers necessary to pass the test?

    70% × 35 = 0.7 × 35 = 7 × 3.5 = 21 + 3.5 = 24.5 = **25**

12. In a school of one hundred and ninety-two pupils, seven-twelfths are boys. How many girls are there?

    192 × 5/12 = 192 ÷ 12 × 5 = (180 ÷ 12 + 12 ÷ 12) × 5
    (15 + 1) × 5 = **80**

Mental arithmetic test 5

1. Four hundred and twenty-four pupils in a year group sit GCSE Maths. If seventy-nine pupils failed to achieve grade C or above, how many pupils did achieve grade C or above?

   424 – 79 = 424 – 100 + 21 (subtract 100 then add back 21)
   = 324 + 21 = **345**

2. The cost of a school trip to France was four hundred and thirty pounds last year. This year the trip will cost eleven percent more. What will be the cost of the trip this year?

   £430 + '11%' = 430 + '10%' + '1%'
   = 430 + 43 + 4.3 = **£477.3**
   (430 × 1.11 on a calculator)

3. GCSE pupils take Triple, Double or Single Science. If three-quarters take the Double Science and one-sixth take Single Science, how many take Triple Science?

   1 (whole) – 3/4 – 1/6 LCD = 12 (twelfths)
   12/12 – 9/12 – 2/12 = **1/12**

4. A school charges six pence per A4 page for photocopying, thirty pence for binding and twenty-five pence for a clear cover. What is the cost of two one-hundred page books bound with clear front and back covers?

   1 book: 6 p × 100 pages = £6 + 30p + 2 × 25p = £6.80
   2 books = **£13.60**

5. What is twenty-two point five percent as a decimal fraction?

   22.5% = 22.5 ÷ 100 = **0.225**

6. The average weight of a class of eleven year old pupils is forty kilograms. What is this in pounds if one kilogram is equivalent to two point two pounds?

   $40 \times 2.2 = 4 \times 22 = $ **88 pounds**

7. A school teacher hires a minibus at fifty pounds per day plus the cost of the petrol used. The minibus uses one litre of fuel for every ten kilometres travelled. If fuel costs one pound and fifty pence per litre, how much would it cost for a one-day round trip of two hundred kilometres?

   1 litre per 10 km = 20 litres per 200 km = $20 \times$ £1.5 = $2 \times$ £15 = £30; £30 + £50 = **£80**

8. The pass mark in a class test is sixty percent. If there are forty-two questions, how many must be answered correctly to pass?

   $60\% \times 42 = 0.6 \times 42 = 6 \times 4.2 = 24 + 1.2 = 25.2 = $ **26**

9. What is zero point zero five multiplied by one thousand?

   $0.05 \times 1000 = $ **50**

10. A school trip requires three forty-seater coaches to hold the pupils and teachers. Two of the coaches are full and the third is three-quarters full. How many teachers went on the trip if there was one teacher for every nine pupils?

    $40 + 40 + 30 = 110$; 1 teacher + 9 pupils = 10 people; teachers = $1/10 \times 110 = $ **11 teachers** (and pupils = 99)

11. A school wildlife pond is four metres in diameter. What is the diameter of the pond on a fifty to one scale drawing?

    4 m $\div$ 50 = 400 cm $\div$ 50 = 800 cm $\div$ 100 = **8 cm**

12. A school day ends at five past three. There are two lessons in the afternoon each lasting fifty minutes with a ten minute break in between. At what time does the first afternoon lesson begin?

    50 min + 50 min + 10 min = 1 hr 50 min
    1505 – 1 hr 50 min = 1505 – 2 hr + 10 min
    = 1305 + 10 = **1315 hrs** (24 hour clock)

Figure 3.1 and 3.2 example answers

1. Food expenditure is the largest sector for girls
2. Appearance is the smallest sector for boys
3. Food expenditure is similar for boys and girls
4. One-quarter of the circle = 25%
5. Boys spend 1/2 × girls on appearance: 1/2 × 1/4 = 1/8

Figure 3.3 example answers

1. 20% are researchers
2. 1/5 are researchers
3. 35% = 35/100 = 7/20
4. 16% = 16/100 = 8/50 = 4/25
5. 0.35 + 0.16 = 0.51
6. 0.2 × 160,000 = 2 × 16,000 = 32,000
7. 16% + 20% – 35% = 1%; 1/100 × 160,000 = 1600
8. 0.09 × 160,000 = 9 x1600 = 10 x1600 – 1600 = 14400
9. Ratio of male to female = 5:1. Total parts = 5 +1 = 6 parts and we have 1 part: 1/6 × 14400 = 2400

Figure 3.4 example answers

1. Longest bar = Maths
2. Fifth longest = Design
3. History = 4%; 4 × 3 = 12% = English

4. Science double = 9%; 2/3 × 9% = 6% = French
5. 10% = 1/10 = 0.1
6. 12% + 13% = 25% = 1/4
7. 10:12 = 5:6
8. 180 × 5/6 = 30 × 5 = 150
9. 12 + 10 + 6 + 8 + 4 + 9 +13 = 62%
10. 100% – 62% = 38% = 0.38

Figure 3.5 example answers

1. 50% × 180 = 90
2. 1/3 × 180 = 60; 60 × 70% = 60 × 0.7 = 6 × 7 = 42
3. 60% × 180 – 50% × 180 = 10% × 180 = 18
4. 54 pupils = 75% = 3/4; so 1/4 is 54 ÷ 3 = 18; 4/4 is 72

Figure 3.6 example answers

1. Level 4 (bar B is longer than bar A)
2. Bar B = 50 – 20 = 30; Bar A = 20 – 0 = 20; B:A = 30:20 = 3:2

Figure 3.7 example answers

1. 140 miles in 3.5 hours = 280 ÷ 7 = 40 mph
2. 2 hr – 1.5 hr = 30 minutes (stationary = no distance travelled = line horizontal)
3. 0 hr = 10.00 hr; 3.5 hr (13.30) – 2 hr (midday) = 1.5 hr distance = 140 – 60 = 80 miles; 80 ÷ 1.5 = 53.3 = 53 mph
4. (3, 120)

Figure 3.8 example answers

1. Chemistry results show the least fluctuation.
2. 450 – 300 = 150
3. 500 – 400 = 100
4. 200; extend the line from 700 in 1990 to 200 by 2000 (or 100 fewer passes every two years = 500 fewer passes in 10 years)

Figure 3.9 example answers

1. 70% read off the y-axis
2. Level 3–8 minus level 5–8 = 95% – 70% = 25%
3. 75% = ¾
4. Level 3–8 minus level 5–8 = 95% – 75% = 20% = 1/5

Figure 3.13 example answers

1. 23 half days = 11.5 days; 72% expected to achieve level 4+
2. Worse = coordinate point is below the line
3. Better = coordinate point is above the line

Figure 3.14 example answers

1. Pupil E lies on a diagonal line that shows equal performance in both tests (equal x and y coordinates)
2. 10 pupils below the diagonal line = better in writing
3. 9 pupils above the diagonal line = better in arithmetic
4. 12 pupils on or above the horizontal line
5. 14 pupils to the right of the horizontal line
6. 11 pupils in the top right-hand corner
7. 5 pupils in the bottom left-hand corner
8. Pupil F is the furthest away from the diagonal line with a difference of 10 marks

Table 3.2 example answers

1. $7 + 6 \times 2 + 5 \times 3 = 7 + 12 + 15 = 34$
2. $34 \div 6 = 5.67$ to 2 dp

Table 3.3 example answers

1. Points = $6 \times 7 = 42 + 3 = 45$
2. Grade B (nearest to 45 points)
3. Grade D ($6 \times 5 + 3 = 30 + 3 = 33$)

4. Grade B = 46 points; 46 = 6 × KS3 level + 3, 46 (– 3) = 6KS3; 43 = 6KS3; KS3 = 43 ÷ 6 = 7.17, ie 7
5. Points = 45 + 45 + 39 = 129; 129 ÷ 3 = 43
6. 45 × 8 = 320 + 40 = 360
7. 92 +160 + 68 = 320; 320 ÷ 8 = 40
8. 5 × 40 + 46 × 2 = 292; 314 – 292 = 22 = grade F

Table 3.4 example answers

1. Read down from C and across from C to find 4
2. Read across from C: 1 + 2 + 4 + 2 = 9 (also see Total column)
3. Read down from A: 2 + 2 + 2 + 1 = 7 (also see Total column)
4. 35 = total for French and total for Spanish (bottom corner)
5. Modal grade for French = most popular grade = grade C (occurs 9 times: 1 + 2 + 4 + 2 = 9: see Total column; note that the answer is C not 9)
6. Grade C or above in Spanish = C + B + A + A* = 9 + 9 + 5 + 4 = 27 pupils
7. 27 ÷ 35 × 100% = 77.1%
8. 10 pupils lie to the left of the diagonal line drawn from A*A* to GG

Figure 3.16 example answers

1. Total the bars: 150 students.
2. Grade C or above = 133; 133 ÷ 150 × 100% = 88.7%
3. Modal = most popular = A-grade
4. Median = (n + 1) ÷ 2 = 151 ÷ 2 = 75.5 (75th to 76th pupil) which goes from ie B grade 44th to 83rd pupil
5. 96% = 0.96; 0.96 × 150 = 144

Figure 3.17 example answers

1. 43 + 25 + 8 + 4 = 80; total = 125; 80 ÷ 125 × 100% = 64%
2. Ratio = 80:45 = 16:9
3. 3 centre bars = 27 + 43 + 25 = 95; 95 ÷ 125 × 100 = 76%

Figure 3.18 example answers

1. 35
2. 46
3. 50
4. 51 – 35 = 16
5. 51 – 46 = 5
6. 51 – 50 = 1
7. 51 – 17 = 34
8. 51 minus E and below = 46 (or read from the table)
9. 34 ÷ 51 = 2 ÷ 3 = 2/3
10. 46 ÷ 51 × 100 = 90.2%
11. Grade B and above = 51 minus grade C and below = 51 – 35 = 16; 16 ÷ 51 × 100 = 31.4%

Figure 3.19 example answers

1. 58
2. 22
3. 58 – 22 = 36
4. 46
5. 140
6. 160 – 140 = 20
7. 160 – 12 = 148

Figure 3.20 example answers

1. 18
2. 20
3. 13
4. 30
5. 100 – 30 = 70 (100 minus those with 16 marks and below); see the answer in 4: 30% achieved 16 or lower so 70% achieved more than 16

Figure 3.23 example answers

1. Maths
2. English ('white line')
3. Science (shortest boxes)
4. Maths
5. English (54% = median = half above and half below)
6. Science (similar length whiskers)
7. 60% (upper quartile starts here)
8. Maths (the range of marks for the top 25% of pupils are shown by the length of the upper quartile whiskers)
9. 80 × 50% = 40 (half of the marks are in the inter-quartile range)
10. English – all three subjects have their upper quartiles (whiskers) extending above 60% but only English has a proportion of the inter-quartile range above 60%

Answers to mock test 1

Question 1

69.8 F = (21 + 40) × 1.8 – 40 = 61 × 1.8 – 40

Question 2

1. True (end of whisker)
2. True (54 – 38 = 16)
3. False (one-quarter of the marks were 38 or below so three-quarters were above 38)

Question 3

1. False (36:32 = 9:8)
2. True (10:45 = 2:9)
3. False (30:50 = 3:5)

Question 4

1. False (the median mark occurs at 50% cumulative frequency)
2. True (the upper quartile occurs at 75% cumulative frequency with a mark of about 70%)
3. True (a mark of 50% has a cumulative frequency of less than 10% so at least 90% achieved a mark of 50% or more)

Question 5

1. True (100% – 89% = 11%)
2. False (we know the percentage but not the actual number)
3. True (A*–G minus A*–C = D, E, F, G = 100% – 92% = 8%; 8% = 8 per 100 = 2 per 25

Question 6

£50. €13 = £10; £200 ÷ £10 = 20; 20 × €13 = €260. €260 – €195 = €65; €65 ÷ €13 = 5; 5 × £10 = £50

Question 7

1. False (A: 0.25 × 400 = 100; B: 0.3 × 330 = 99)
2. True (25% + 13% + 28% = 66%; 0.66 × 400 = 264)
3. True (30% + 9% + 33% = 72%; 25% + 13% + 28% = 66%)

Question 8

1. True (75 × 3 + 77 + 79) ÷ 5 = 381 ÷ 5 = 76.2
2. False (73.2 × 5 = 366 = total; 366 – 71 – 73 – 74 – 75 = 73%)
3. False (median: 86, 86, 86, 87, 87)

Question 9

Arithmetic (36 ÷ 40 = 90%; 43 ÷ 50 = 86%; 54 ÷ 60 = 90%) ie reading and arithmetic have the highest scores. Smallest range: arithmetic 29/60 = 48% (Reading 21/40 = 53%)

Question 10

12.6 kg (21 cm × 30 cm = 0.21 m × 0.3 m = 0.063 m^2; 0.063 m^2 × 80 g/m^2 = 5.04 g; 5.04 × 500 × 5 ÷1000 = 12.6 kg)

Question 11

1. True (for all five percentage intervals)
2. True (40+ interval displays the largest jump for 2000–2004)
3. False (in 2004, 90% of the pupils achieved KS2 Level 4+ in schools where <10% of the pupils were entitled to free school meals)

Question 12

1. 80% (8 out of 10 pupils)
2. 2/3 (6 out of 9; check line by line)
3. 60% (6 out of 10; check line by line)

Question 13
0815 (0845 – 30 = 0815; using the swift ferry)

Question 14
2004 (school is slightly more than 10% above local authority)

Question 15
Test 1: 53% ($70 \times 0.5 + 36 \times 0.5 = 35 + 18 = 53$)
Test 2: 54% ($60 \times 0.7 + 40 \times 0.3 = 42 + 12 = 54$)

Question 16
9/20 (45% boys = 45/100 = 9/20)

Answers to mock test 2

Question 1

1. False (boys did better than girls in maths in 2006)
2. True (boys: 55 to 60; 5/55 = 9%; girls 71 to 75; 4/71 = 5.6%)
3. True (2006 to 2007: boys +2%; girls +0%)

Question 2

43 (1 in 4; remainder = 3/4 =129; 1/4 = 3/4 ÷ 3; 129 ÷ 3 = 43)

Question 3

71% (weighting: 75% × 0.6 + 65% × 0.4 = 45 + 26 = 71%)

Question 4

19.8 (PTR = 170 ÷ (1 + 7 + 15/25) = 170 ÷ (8 + 0.6) = 170 ÷ 8.6)

Question 5

1. Pupil E (is on the median line at 25 points)
2. Pupil P (is on the upper quartile at 28 points; ie 25% of pupils have higher marks and 75% have lower marks)
3. Pupils L (is on the lower quartile at 26 points)

Question 6

£40 (£80 × 4.25 zl/£ = 340 zl; 340 zl – 250 zl = 90 zl; 90 zl ÷ 4.50 zl/£ = £20; £20 + unconverted £20 = £40)

Question 7

1.04 m (32 × 2 + 19 × 2 + 2 = 64 + 38 + 2 = 104 cm = 1.04 m)

Question 8

£10.75 (176 × 1.06 + (84 + 20) × 1.1) = £300.96; £300.96 ÷ 28 = £10.75

Question 9

C (two bars have the same height and two bars have different heights = A or C pie charts; longest bar to shortest bar = 3:1 = C)

Question 10

1150 (181 × 5 = 905; yr 11 = 905 – (185+184+181+180) = 175; yr 11: yr 12 = 7:5 = 175:125 (common factor of 25). Completing the table gives: total = 905 + 125 + 120 = 1150

Question 11

1. False (half not most; the median is at 7 hours)
2. True (10% CF is at 4 hours)
3. True (the lower quartile/25% CF is at about 5¾ hours)

Question 12

B highest; E lowest (convert each to a percentage: A = 5.3%; B = 14%; C = 11.1%; D = 6%; E = 5%; F = 6.8%)

Question 13

1. True (two students on the top line with <52 GCSE points)
2. True (14 out of 21 students have <52 GCSE points)
3. False (one student has 52 GCSE points)

Question 14

0845 (5 miles = 8 kilometres so 50 miles = 80 kilometres; 300 km ÷ 80 km/hr = 30 ÷ 8 hr = 3 6/8 hours = 3 hours 45 min. Departs at 1230 – 3 hr 45 = 1230 – 4 hr + 15 min = 0845 hours)

Question 15

Q (mean number of pupils with A* to C grades for the three classes = (18 +18 + 15) ÷ 3 = 51 ÷ 3 = 17 pupils; mode = most frequent grade = C (27 pupils); Q = mean 17 and mode C)

Question 16

B (B = 0.4 or 40%; with to without ratios: A = 250:700 (0.36); B = 100:250 (0.4); C = 150:400 (0.375); D = 50:200 = 0.25)

Glossary

Accuracy
Of a calculated value, the degree of closeness to the actual value.
see also decimal place, rounding

Algebra
The use of letters and symbols in place of numbers to represent the structure of a formula or relationship between numbers.
eg $y = mx + c$

Arithmetical operation
A function performed on two or more 'input' numbers to create a new number, for example addition, subtraction, multiplication or division.
see also BIDMAS

Bar chart
A statistical graph where data is displayed as a series of vertical or horizontal bars; can be grouped or stacked.

BIDMAS
The order in which arithmetical operations should be performed. Brackets first, then indices ('powers'), followed by division and multiplication and finally addition and subtraction.

Cohort
A statistical term used to define a population.
eg this year's GCSE maths cohort

Conversion
An exchange from one unit to another.
eg pence to pounds, kilometres to metres, minutes to hours

Correlation
The strength of a relationship between two variables, such as grade in GCSE maths versus QTS results.

Cumulative frequency
The sum of the frequencies of an event recorded at different stages, from the beginning to the current position.

Decimal fraction
A number less than 1, where a decimal point precedes the tenth, hundredth and thousandth, etc.
eg 0.732

Decimal number
A number that contains both a whole number and a decimal fraction.
eg 3.75

Decimal place (dp)
The number of digits to the right of a decimal point in a decimal number.
eg 2.75 rounded to 1dp = 2.8

Denominator
The bottom number of a fraction.

Distribution
A statistical term that describes the spread of the data.

Drag and drop questions
An on-screen test format. Here you click on the correct answer, then drag it to its correct location.

Equation
A mathematical statement where two sides are shown to be equal to each other.
eg $a = b + c$

Formula
Similar to an equation, but often identifies a rule.
eg to convert Centigrade to Fahrenheit, $F = 1.8C + 32$.

Fraction
Part of a whole; the denominator (bottom number) is the number of equal parts that the numerator (top) is divided into.

Frequency
A measure of the number of times that something occurs.

Greater than symbol
The symbol >
eg x is greater than five: $x > 5$
see also less than symbol

Histogram
A statistical chart similar to a bar chart, but showing continuous data (such as age ranges) rather than discrete data (such as colours).

Integer
A positive or negative whole number, or zero.

Interquartile range
The difference between the upper quartile and the lower quartile, which represents the middle 50 per cent of the data.

KS
In education, Key Stages. KS1 = ages 4 to 7; KS2 = ages 7 to 11; KS3 = ages 11 to 14 and KS4 = ages 14 to 16.

Less than symbol
The symbol <
eg x is less than five: x <5
see also greater than symbol

Line graph
Data is plotted as a series of points joined by a line. Useful for showing trends, ie increases and decreases.

Lower quartile
In statistics, the mark below which one-quarter of the marks lie (the bottom 25 per cent of the range); 75 per cent of the marks lie above it.

Mean
A value found by dividing the total of all of a group of numbers by how many numbers there are in that group; the 'average'.
see also median, mode

Measurement
The determination of length, weight, volume or any other quantity.

Median
The middle number in a group of numbers that have been placed in numerical order, from smallest to the largest.
see also mean, mode

Mental arithmetic
Maths calculations worked out without using a calculator.

Mode
The value that occurs the most often in a group of numbers.
see also mean, median

More than symbol
same as greater than symbol

Multiple choice questions
A test format. This offers several alternative answers where only one is correct.
eg 'How many degrees make a full circle?'
a) 180 degrees
b) 360 degrees
c) 720 degrees

NOR
Number on roll: the number of pupils enrolled at a school.

Numerator
The top number of a fraction.

On-screen questions
A test format. The answers are inputted using the mouse or keyboard.

Percentage
A fraction with a denominator of 100; a fraction expressed in hundredths.

Percentage change
The change in a value (increase or decrease) divided by the original value and multiplied by 100 per cent.

Percentage point
One per cent, used to express the difference between two percentages.
eg the difference between 50 per cent and 60 per cent is 10 percentage points

Percentile

When results are placed in order of rank and divided into 100 equal parts, the value at or below which that percentage of results falls.
eg the 70th percentile of test marks = the mark at or below which 70 per cent of results fall

Pie chart

A statistical graph in which a full circle (360 degrees) equals 100 per cent of the data. So half of the circle = 180 degrees = 50 per cent of the data; a quarter of the circle = 90 degrees = 25 per cent, etc.

Prediction

The forecasting or extrapolation of pupils' future results based on current performance.

Quartile

One of four quarter parts that results are divided into, by the 25th, 50th and 75th percentiles.

Range

The difference between the highest value and the lowest value in a data spread.

Ratio

Two or more quantities compared as either whole numbers or fractions.
eg 2 parts to 5 parts; 2:5 = 2/7 and 5/7

Raw score

A result showing the actual marks that the person scored on a particular test.
see also standardised score

Reading age

In a reading test, the national average score for a child. For example, most 10-year-olds will have a reading age of 10.

Rounding
A method for simplifying numbers to the required level of accuracy, to the nearest 10, 100, 1000, etc.
eg 178 rounded up to the nearest 10 = 180; to the nearest hundred = 200, etc.

SATs
Standardized Assessments Tasks; tests set at the end of each year to show pupil progress.

Scale
1. A graduation mark on an axis or ruler.
2. A way of showing how one measurement relates to another, eg on a map or chart.

eg 1:50,000 (1 cm = 0.5 km)

Scatter graph
A statistical graph plotting paired or related data, eg height and weight, to show whether or not a correlation exists.

Sector
A 'wedge' or part of a circle, as used to represent a percentage in a pie chart.
see also pie chart

Single response questions
A test format. Enter the correct answer in the way requested.
eg if asked to 'express the amount to the nearest pound', for '£10.75' you would enter '£11'

Standardised score
A raw score that has been converted to take account of some other factor, eg age.
see also raw score

Table
A way of displaying data using a grid.

Tally chart
A table that is used to record the frequency of data.

Trend
A pattern, sequence or series; the general direction in which something is tending to move, eg upwards or downwards.

Two-way table
A table that is useful for comparing pupil performance in two subjects or in two different years.

Unity
The number one (1).

ALSO AVAILABLE FROM KOGAN PAGE

ISBN: 978 0 7494 4969 8
Paperback 2008

ISBN: 978 0 7494 5229 2
Paperback 2008

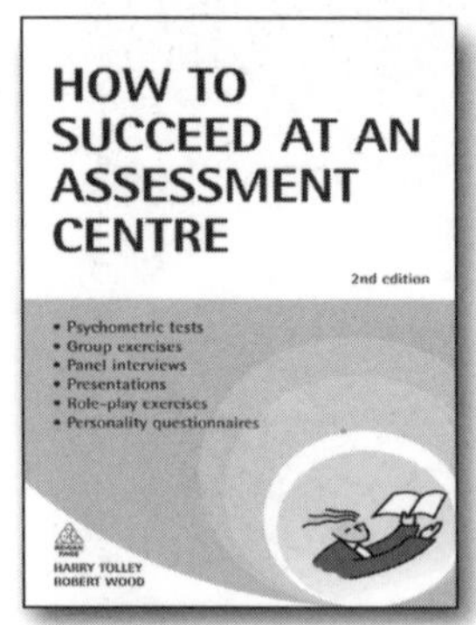

ISBN: 978 0 7494 4421 1
Paperback 2005

ISBN: 978 0 7494 5064 9
Paperback 2007

Order online now at www.koganpage.com

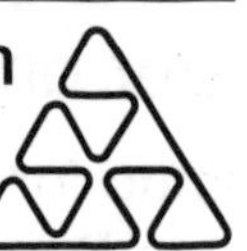

Sign up for regular e-mail updates on new Kogan Page books in your interest area

ALSO AVAILABLE FROM KOGAN PAGE

ISBN: 978 0 7494 5106 6
Paperback 2007

ISBN: 978 0 7494 4852 3
Paperback 2007

ISBN: 978 0 7494 4954 4
Paperback 2007

ISBN: 978 0 7494 5165 3
Paperback 2008

Order online now at www.koganpage.com

Sign up for regular e-mail updates on new Kogan Page books in your interest area

ALSO AVAILABLE FROM KOGAN PAGE

ISBN: 978 0 7494 4819 6
Paperback 2006

ISBN: 978 0 7494 4931 5
Paperback 2007

ISBN: 978 0 7494 5237 7
Paperback 2008

ISBN: 978 0 7494 3887 6
Paperback 2003

Order online now at www.koganpage.com

Sign up for regular e-mail updates on new Kogan Page books in your interest area